A WAR OF WORDS

C. P. Mayhew by Fred May

A WAR OF WORDS
A Cold War Witness

Christopher Mayhew

Recorded and Edited by Lyn Smith

Foreword by the Lord Jenkins of Hillhead

BLOOMSBURY ACADEMIC
LONDON • NEW YORK • OXFORD • NEW DELHI • SYDNEY

BLOOMSBURY ACADEMIC
Bloomsbury Publishing Plc
50 Bedford Square, London, WC1B 3DP, UK
1385 Broadway, New York, NY 10018, USA
29 Earlsfort Terrace, Dublin 2, Ireland

BLOOMSBURY, BLOOMSBURY ACADEMIC and the Diana logo
are trademarks of Bloomsbury Publishing Plc

First published in Great Britain 1998 by I. B. Tauris
This paperback edition published in 2021

Copyright © Lyn Smith and the Estate of Christopher Mayhew, 1998

Lyn Smith and the Estate of Christopher Mayhew have asserted their rights under the Copyright, Designs and Patents Act, 1988, to be identified as Author of this work.

All rights reserved. No part of this publication may be reproduced or transmitted in any form or by any means, electronic or mechanical, including photocopying, recording, or any information storage or retrieval system, without prior permission in writing from the publishers.

Bloomsbury Publishing Plc does not have any control over, or responsibility for, any third-party websites referred to or in this book. All internet addresses given in this book were correct at the time of going to press. The author and publisher regret any inconvenience caused if addresses have changed or sites have ceased to exist, but can accept no responsibility for any such changes.

A catalogue record for this book is available from the British Library.

A catalog record for this book is available from the Library of Congress.

ISBN: HB: 978-1-8606-3160-8
PB: 978-1-3501-8219-6

Typeset by Oxford Publishing Services, Oxford

To find out more about our authors and books visit www.bloomsbury.com and sign up for our newsletters.

Contents

Acronyms and Abbreviations	vi
Foreword by the Lord Jenkins of Hillhead	vii
Introduction by Lyn Smith	ix

1.	Does the Future Work? My Disillusionment with the Soviets	1
2.	Propaganda and the Workers' Paradise	14
3.	The Cultural Cold War	48
4.	Against 'Peace'	80
5.	Stalin's Foreign Friends	98
6.	Cold War: Reflections, Doubts and Some Regrets	111

Notes   117

Appendix 1: Extracts of Memorandum, C. Mayhew to E. Bevin, urging establishment of IRD   120
Appendix 2: Memorandum by the Secretary of State for Foreign Affairs   123
Appendix 3: Extracts from Circular 0121   128
Appendix 4: Forced Labour in the Soviet Union   129
Appendix 5: Letter Christopher Mayhew to Mr A. A. Arutiunian, 31 October 1947   137

Bibliography   141
Index   143

Acronyms and Abbreviations

ACCT	Association of Cinematograph, Television and Allied Technicians
BEF	British Expeditionary Force
BSFS	British–Soviet Friendship Society
CBS	Columbian Broadcasting System
CDS	Campaign for Democratic Socialism
CFM	Council of Foreign Ministers
CMD	Campaign for Multilateral Disarmament
CND	Campaign for Nuclear Disarmament
EB	Ernest Bevin
FO	Foreign Office
IRD	Information Research Department
IUS	International Union of Students
KGB	Komitet Gosudarstvennoi Bezopasnosti (*Russian*: Committee of State Security)
MI5	Military Intelligence, section five (British counter-intelligence agency)
NATO	North Atlantic Treaty Organization
PLP	Parliamentary Labour Party
SCR	Society for Cultural Relations
SDP	Social Democratic Party
SRC	Soviet Relations Committee
SS	Secretary of State
Tass	Telegrafnoye Agentstvo Sovetskovo Soyuza (Russian news agency)
TUC	Trades Union Congress
ULF	University Labour Federation
WFDY	World Federation of Democratic Youth
WFTU	World Federation of Trade Unions

Foreword
The Lord Jenkins of Hillhead

This is a fascinating fragment of autobiography (but a fragment even more in the sense of dealing with a particular aspect of his life than of being unfinished) by a man of exceptional energy and courage. Christopher Mayhew, although he changed parties (from Labour to Liberal) in 1974, retained a remarkably consistent political position throughout the nearly sixty years for which I knew him. He was always an anti-Conservative and anti-Communist Social Democrat. This book is not about his anti-Conservatism but about his anti-Communism, and in this, as in his other beliefs, he was always an activist. He never just rested on his convictions but always did something about them.

Yet in his anti-communism he was never an obsessive or even a conventional 'cold warrior', not a John Foster Dulles or a Senator Knowland. It was always a genuine *détente* rather than confrontation or brinkmanship which he sought. But he was convinced that that could not be attained unless the West at least kept its end up in the propaganda battle. As a young Foreign Office junior minister, he was therefore instrumental in the setting up of a new propaganda venture which sheltered under the somewhat vapid title of the Information Research Department (IRD). It was not, however, clandestine and it was far from vapid in performance. It led to British embassies entering into the game of what would now be called 'instant rebuttal' of Soviet denunciations. Mayhew wanted the IRD to promote positive propaganda for Western social democracy (i.e. the achievements of the British Labour government) as well as the undermining of Soviet claims. But he found that a bridge too far for the Foreign Office and had to be content with establishing an effective and long-lasting but more negative agency.

In the 14 years of opposition, which then intervened before he

Foreword

returned to a brief and final couple of years in middle-rank office (ended by an arguably perverse but certainly principled resignation), Mayhew devoted himself to another aspect of the promotion of the 'level playing field', which he saw as essential to healthy relations between Russia and Britain, and indeed with the West as a whole. The Soviet habit had been to try to conduct cultural relations and all others which were not strictly governmental through Communist front organizations, of which the most prominent was the British–Soviet Friendship Society (BSFS). This aroused suspicion in non-fellow travelling Britons and led the Russians who participated to believe that the 'Red' Dean of Canterbury and politicians such as D. N. Pritt and Konni Zilliacus were the most representative figures in British public life.

Mayhew, in association with Fitzroy Maclean and a few others, waged a persistent and on the whole successful battle to correct this. Substantially as a result of his activities the BSFS was pushed into a corner and the much more reputable Britain–USSR Association (with Attlee as president and several Conservative MPs among its officers) came to the centre of the stage in its place.

The book is largely an account of these struggles. It is self-assured in the sense that Mayhew, like Gladstone in this respect, was never diverted from a course by the thought that it might attract sophisticated disapproval. Neither of them feared ridicule. But the book is not self-righteous or lacking in self-criticism. It is a fine testament from a man who, after a golden youth, did not achieve all the glittering prizes which were predicted for him, largely because he always preferred the pursuit of truth, as he sometimes awkwardly saw it, to career advancement.

Roy Jenkins, 30 December 1997

Introduction

This book had its inception in 1980 with the publication of an article for the LSE journal *Millennium* on the Information Research Department (IRD), the existence of which had been recently brought to light by the journalists David Leigh and Richard Fletcher.[1] At that time, just after the Soviet intervention in Afghanistan, the cold war was entering a new phase. The IRD was a very sensitive subject and few of those known to have been involved with the department during the years of its operation (1948–77) were prepared to talk openly about it, let alone go on the record. Indeed, its very existence was denied by the Foreign Office functionaries I approached.

Christopher Mayhew was an exception: the IRD was his 'baby' and he was proud of it. Not only was he willing to answer questions about its origins and early development – in which he had been instrumental – but he was also generous with his private papers and gave me every encouragement. Mayhew and I kept in touch through our mutual political interests and when the cold war ended in 1990, I supported his efforts to push for the release of IRD documents through his connections with the Foreign Office. The first batch of papers relating to the critical year of 1948 were released in 1995. These were received, in the main, with a spate of criticism about the IRD generally, and Mayhew in particular. He was dismayed by what he perceived as a lack of comprehension of the cold war climate of the postwar years by his critics, many of whom were, as he argued, of a generation reared in more gentle climes and unwilling or unable to appreciate the exigencies of earlier times. He therefore wished to give a full version of events as he saw them and invited me to cooperate.

As well as dealing with the origins and development of the IRD, Mayhew wished to cover another, far less controversial, organization he helped to found – the Soviet Relations Committee (SRC).[2] This aimed to take over from and marginalize the communist-led friendship

Introduction

societies which, prior to 1954, had organized cultural exchanges between Britain and the Soviet Union. The aims of this 'cultural cold war' were at first purely political, and ideologically driven; but experiencing and enjoying contacts with Soviet artists and musicians, his motivation changed and he began to doubt the morality of using culture as a propaganda weapon.

Mayhew would not have shirked the title of cold warrior as applying to his role in the early cold war years. But in fact, he was no dogmatist. In the early 1970s, he was quick to perceive the changes occurring in the Soviet empire, realizing that the maintenance of a cold-warrior stance was outdated and mischievous. Appalled by the 'evil empire' rhetoric of President Ronald Reagan and his 'Star Wars' programme, and the Soviet response of 'Operation Ryan', he saw the world being brought to the brink of nuclear catastrophe. With his keen eye on East/West events, as time went on he saw opportunities for serious dialogue on disengagement from Europe, even the case – then anathema – for German reunification. He argued publicly and unsuccessfully that these opportunities should be seized, suffering ridicule and some ostracism in the process.

Methodology consisted of a combination of interviews, recorded cassettes, documents and discussions. Mayhew set firm parameters and always had complete control. My role was to probe, transcribe, edit and redraft; but he always insisted that the content reflected accurately his own recollections and perceptions. He died in January 1997 having just dictated the final chapter, which is here quoted verbatim. Had he lived, with the final probing of material and edit of the book that we had anticipated, it would possibly have been different – more substantial with greater analysis of the cold war, particularly the role of ideology and propaganda during the Stalinist era. Given contemporary controversy over IRD, I also hoped to encourage him to confront some of the more questionable aspects of the department's activities.

As it stands, this is the testimony of a politician whose life spanned the entire course of the cold war, in its broadest time-span definition – a man who from being one of Lenin's 'useful idiots' became one of Britain's most vigorous and combative anti-communist campaigners. At the very heart of events in the UN, Mayhew perceived that the

Introduction

Western democracies, and Britain in particular, were coming under attack from a highly sophisticated and extensive Soviet propaganda network, and at a time when there was a power vacuum in Europe, and when the newly-independent countries of the British Empire were vulnerable to Soviet penetration. For Mayhew, this was intolerable; he had no doubts about the total evil of communism and the rightness of social democracy and he set out to do something about it.

Mayhew's witness also highlights the role of Britain in the cold war. Until recently this has been minimized or ignored, with the debate being cast mainly in US/Soviet bipolar terms. Mayhew's role in the IRD highlights the ideological causes of the cold war in its Stalinist stage, and demonstrates that it was Britain that went on the counteroffensive against Soviet propaganda in a highly organized and aggressive manner, well before the USA had its CIA propaganda machine up and running. Mayhew takes contemporary American authors to task for continuing the trend of marginalizing Britain. He would have been heartened by J. L. Gaddis's latest book on the cold war where Britain's early role as well as the significance of the ideological factor are acknowledged.[3]

I profoundly regret that Christopher Mayhew did not live to see his work published. My thanks to Norman Reddaway, Lady Mayhew, the Reverend David Mayhew and Dr Lester Crook, of I.B.Tauris Ltd for the staunch support they have given in bringing the book to publication.

Lyn Smith, May 1998

Notes

1. Smith, Lyn, 'Covert British Propaganda: The Information Research Department 1917–1977', *Millennium: Journal of International Studies*, vol. 9, no. 1, 1980.
2. Later the Great Britain–USSR Association. Today the British–Russia Centre.
3. Gaddis, J. L., *We Now Know: Rethinking Cold War History* (Clarendon Press, Oxford, 1997).

Chapter 1
Does the Future Work? My Disillusionment with the Soviets

But what was Russia really like? It must surely be a better society than ours, being its exact opposite; or so it seemed to my school friend David Nenk and myself. We were teenage socialists, rebels against the conservative traditions of our public school, Haileybury. David was brilliantly clever, sardonic, Jewish. In his spare time he was starting to write a history of utopias. We decided to visit Russia together. In the summer of 1935, we paid £15 each for a ten-day Intourist trip to Moscow and Leningrad. We were determined to discover for ourselves the truth about the Soviet Union: namely that it was a socialist utopia hitherto hidden from us by a blanket of capitalist propaganda.

David equipped himself, in a phenomenally short time, with a working knowledge of Russian, and we joined a small Soviet passenger ship at London Bridge, dressed in a rather proletarian style, which we judged would help us mix easily with the workers of Leningrad and Moscow.

Our first surprise was the state of the ship's lavatories. By the standards of reactionary capitalist countries, they were so filthy as to be unusable. Why was this? This was a question we should have asked ourselves persistently. We might then have discovered some part of the truth about the Soviet Union. But we didn't do it. The state of the lavatories was inconsistent with everything we had read about socialism. It was obviously an accident, a hangover from a past age, the kind of thing that would only matter to people from sheltered bourgeois homes such as ours. The ship's crew, dedicated to a high ideal, could not be expected to pamper people such as ourselves.

Similar reasons, we felt, also explained the surprising reluctance of the workers of Moscow and Leningrad to talk to us. Wherever we went, we tried earnestly to engage them in conversation. We failed. They would look at us, note that we were foreigners, and hastily walk away.

At that time, of course, with the Stalinist purges at their height, it was dangerous for a Soviet citizen to be seen talking to a foreigner. Avoiding contact with David and myself was simply a necessary act of self-preservation. For our part, we understood nothing of the horrors of Stalinist oppression, which we assumed to be a fiction of capitalist propaganda. Having conscientiously studied Joseph Stalin's proposed new constitution, our eyes were fixed on the new liberal era which, we felt sure, it would usher in. Our failure to communicate with the Soviet workers, peasants and intelligentsia was plainly due to our own shortcomings. Why should they be bothered with ignorant tourists from capitalist countries? And, of course, it was always possible that they could not understand David's Russian.

Earnestly, eagerly, herded together with other foreign visitors, we followed our guides round the Intourist trail. We visited a collective farm, some factories, a crèche, a school. Some things we saw pleased us: here were the proofs that socialism worked. Other things we saw disappointed us: this showed that the vestiges of capitalism could not all be eradicated overnight. Knowing little or nothing of the factories of any other country, we found it easy to wax enthusiastic about Soviet factories, and if some of them did seem below standard, this simply showed that – contrary to the insinuations of capitalist propaganda – Intourist showed the bad side as well as the good.

Apart from our Intourist guides, double talkers and double thinkers to a man, only one Soviet citizen deliberately entered into conversation with us during our tour. This was a quiet-spoken man who accosted us in Gorky Street and asked us if we would like to buy roubles at ten times the official rate. At the official rate, the shortest tram ride cost half a crown. We eagerly agreed to exchange £3 worth, and were given an appointment at a bedroom in the Metropole Hotel. I knocked at the door at the stated time and when the door was opened, said quite loudly, 'I've come for those roubles.' I was astonished by his terrified appeal for silence.

Looking back, I feel thoroughly ashamed of my obtuseness on this

Does the Future Work?

visit. Our British system of society seemed so detestable that I simply could not believe that its exact antithesis could be even worse. Though I did not know it at the time, several of our colleagues on our package tour were communists or fellow-travellers, and at least one later became a Soviet agent. When I leant out of my hotel bedroom window in Moscow to take a forbidden photograph of the Kremlin, the person kindly holding my legs was Anthony Blunt.

David was less easily taken in by this trip than I was. Yet we were both deceived. How could this happen? How could the same weird misjudgements be made by so many of our generation? When David and I went on – he to Cambridge, I to Oxford – we found our Stalinist illusions widely shared there.

The political starting point for alert young people in the mid-1930s was the abysmal state of our class-ridden society. We resented, genuinely and rightly, the economic and social injustices of the time and were willing to support drastic measures to remove them. Many of us too had come from public schools where we had rebelled against oppressive and hierarchical regimes. I have described elsewhere my own rather colourful schoolboy rebellion and conversion to socialism.[2]

At about this time, the Oxford Union debated a motion 'that this House prefers the Red Flag to the Union Jack'. I spoke in support of the Red Flag, and the university paper, *Isis*, reported perceptively: 'We are forced to the strange conclusion that it is in the interests of Conservatism that the public schools be destroyed before they turn loose too many bitter young socialists and communists. If the latter wish to make the country a communist state, they really should insist that everyone is sent to public school.' About my own speech, the *Isis* recorded, 'Mr Mayhew was not on his best form and had altogether an unhappy evening.'

Revolt by our generation against the wretched state of our society was natural enough – even predictable. Placing our hopes of salvation on Stalin's Russia was almost incomprehensible.

True – we lacked reliable information. Stalin had largely sealed off the Soviet Union from the outside world. Soviet censorship allowed out only a thin trickle of information, all filtered through its news agency Tass and by state-controlled radio and film. Even this, however, was enough to make an impact on immature minds. At Oxford, my left-wing friends and I would often go to a small cinema in Beaumont Street, to watch films with titles like *The Successes of Collective Farming* or *The Conquest of Illiteracy* and so on. I can still remember stirring pictures of combine harvesters working smoothly in the sunlight on collective farms, of Stalin greeting Young Pioneers with a hug, of children hurrying happily to school.

Moreover, many more mature people had visited the Soviet Union from the West, as David Nenk and I had done, and returned with their illusions intact. This was true even of the famous and respected social scientists Sidney and Beatrice Webb, who had returned from the Soviet Union to write a substantial book eulogizing the Stalinist state as 'A New Civilization'.

Then there was the clarity and persuasiveness of the Marxist message as it was presented to us. History was a struggle between economic classes. In our era, that meant a struggle between the capitalist class and the working class, the exploited and the exploiters, the rich and the poor, the old established and the new. Capitalism was doomed: the recent world slump proved it. Since it robbed the workers of their due of 'surplus value', capitalism could not sell its output, and thus created unemployment at home and a dangerous struggle for markets abroad. This, in its turn, led to colonial oppression and war.

These basic Marxist dogmas were simple and clear and seemed logical enough to our immature minds. Moreover, they helped to explain why intelligent people, such as our tutors, argued against Marxism: they had all had a traditional bourgeois education and belonged to the capitalist class.

So I was at this time quite convinced of the social and economic claims of Soviet communism. But on one issue, I did show a degree of common sense. I did realize that, whatever the future might hold, for the moment the Soviet political system was a dictatorship. In common with many idealistic socialists, I did not attach much importance to this at the time, believing, naively, that with rising living standards the worst of the oppression would fade away.

However, this did not stop me arguing that for the moment the Soviet state was a dictatorship; and in a shipboard debate on the way

Does the Future Work?

home, in face of strong opposition, I made a spirited attack on the lack of freedom in the Soviet Union. Strangely, this reassuring information was given to me, more than 30 years later, long after I had forgotten it, by MI5. My informant was Mr Peter Wright, author of the notorious book *Spycatcher*, which the British government of the time had tried so hard, and failed so conspicuously, to suppress. Wright was then a well-dressed, rather handsome man, looking fully at home in the Oxford and Cambridge Club, where he had invited me to meet him. He began by asking me if I could explain why my name had appeared on the back of an invitation card that had been collected from Guy Burgess's flat when he fled to the Soviet Union in 1951. I asked why I had not been asked this many years earlier. He replied that by an oversight MI5 had failed, until now, to examine the back of the invitation card. I replied bluntly that I did not believe this. Without arguing the point, Wright hurried on to question me – or was he interrogating me? – about my trip to the Soviet Union in 1935. Who had been my fellow passengers? I mentioned Anthony Blunt and his brother Wilfrid, Harry Pollitt (then general secretary of the Communist Party), and one or two others I remembered. However, Wright was not satisfied. Eventually, he suggested to me a name I had forgotten, and I confirmed that he had been a member of the party. It was then that Wright informed me, somewhat to my relief, that on the voyage home I had made an anti-Stalinist speech.

At the time, I was astonished that MI5 should show such interest in our 1935 visit, but later I saw a likely explanation. Although I could not know this, the interview was taking place shortly after Anthony Blunt had turned queen's evidence. Blunt would then have surrendered to MI5 the papers he himself had purloined unobtrusively from Guy Burgess's flat, as a member of the MI5 search party. These would have included the invitation card. Blunt would also have informed his interrogators that I was a member of the Party, no doubt arousing some suspicion of myself.

Strangely enough, it was Anthony's brother Wilfrid who started my return to political sanity. Wilfrid was the art master at Haileybury, and on his return he sent me an article he had written in the school magazine describing a Soviet factory we had visited together. A sensitive person of artistic temperament, despising politics, he had seen the factory with the eye of truth and wrote about it as it really was. He said it was dirty, overcrowded, noisy and old-fashioned, and the workers were badly dressed and looked miserably poor and oppressed. This seemed to me heartless treachery, and I was deeply shocked; but I remember forcing myself to read the article again, carefully, and then again, until finally compelled to acknowledge that what this political ignoramus had written was true and that the opinions of the factory that I myself had formed – I, the expert, the politician, the dedicated student of communism – were almost certainly rubbish. This was an important moment for me. I began to realize how badly my perceptions of the Soviet Union had been distorted by self-persuasion.

I visited Wilfrid many years later, in the Surrey village of Compton, where he was the director of the Watts' Gallery. We reminisced, among other things, about the Russian trip. Was Anthony already at that time a communist? Wilfrid emphatically denied it. He said that Anthony had spent almost all his time in Moscow and Leningrad visiting art galleries, as he himself had done. I said that a good friend of mine, on an official visit to the Soviet Union, had been photographed in bed with a Russian boy and subsequently blackmailed. Had this happened to Anthony? Wilfrid denied it. He insisted that he himself had no idea that Anthony was a Soviet spy until the fact became public. He guessed that Anthony had been seduced and recruited by his fellow homosexual, Guy Burgess, whom he described as dangerously charming and persuasive.

Once disillusioned, everything Soviet appeared to me in a new light, and I became increasingly anti-Marxist. My academic work helped in the process. My economics tutor was Roy Harrod (later Sir), already world famous as the collaborator and interpreter of John Maynard Keynes. He made me study Keynes's celebrated general theory, and I began to see that mass unemployment might be abolished without resorting to 'the common ownership of the means of production, distribution and exchange' – the drastic remedy demanded by Clause IV of the Labour Party's constitution. This carried me a long step forward away from Marxism.

My philosophy tutor, the eminent moral philosopher, Michael Foster,

Does the Future Work?

also helped to turn me away from Marxism, but by accident. Taciturn, gloomy and inarticulate, he directed me to read the works of René Descartes, John Locke, George Berkeley, David Hume and Immanuel Kant, and I obediently learned off as much as I could stomach of the arguments of these famous thinkers. But what were they arguing about? What did 'philosophy' *mean*? What was it *for*? I could make no sense of it, and Michael Foster could not or would not help me. He sucked an empty pipe and looked enigmatic. However, enlightenment was at hand. Browsing one day in Blackwells, I came across a small book in the fashionable new yellow Gollancz jacket called *Language, Truth and Logic*. Excitingly, it was by somebody still alive, a Christ Church don I had actually met, Professor A. J. Ayer. It cost only 3s. 6d. and I bought it.

It was clear, concise and persuasive, and revealed, to my immense satisfaction, that the works of Descartes, Locke, Berkeley, Hume and Kant – indeed all metaphysics, all theology and all moral philosophy – were a load of rubbish. I was enthralled. The scales fell from my eyes. Now at last I knew the Truth. The Truth was: general statements not capable of being empirically verified (at least in principle) were either tautological or meaningless.

This was liberation indeed. I became an ardent logical positivist. What precisely was the meaning of the terms these famous thinkers used? When Marxists argued that labour was the source of value, what exactly did they mean by 'value'? If development in history and nature was the product of a struggle of opposites – of 'thesis' and 'antithesis' leading to 'synthesis' – what exactly did they mean by 'opposites'? If capitalism was the 'opposite' of feudalism, how could it also be the 'opposite' of socialism?

I soon discovered that even the brightest of my Marxist acquaintances had no answers to questions such as these. In fact, they had not thought about them. They held to Marxist dogma as an article of faith, much as religious undergraduates held to theological dogmas. They were also hard put to supply specific instances of the generalizations they so readily advanced. We argued endlessly, for example, about whether a Labour government, despite the teachings of Lenin, would be able to build socialism peacefully. Would not the capitalist class resort to violence rather than have the instruments of power snatched from its grasp? I myself thought this most unlikely and on one occasion read a paper to this effect to an earnest study group. My most telling point was a quotation from Karl Marx himself declaring that in Britain, though in no other country, a peaceful transition to socialism might be possible. But other sacred texts were tossed around from the works of Lenin, Harold Laski and John Strachey (then a leading communist dialectician) arguing the opposite. Eventually, I was inspired to ask my opponents for the names of three members of the British ruling class who might resort to armed force against an elected government. There was silence at this point, while my Marxist opponents tried, without success, to think of three real, live, capitalists who could plausibly be visualized as arresting Clement Attlee and shooting down members of the Christ Church Socialist Study Group.

My anti-communist views were also strengthened by experience of communist political tactics. Soon after I joined it, the social-democratic Labour Club merged with the openly communist October Club. This led to bitter struggles within the new organization, and I found myself leading a small but resolute anti-communist faction. It all started at a meeting of the Christ Church branch of the Labour Club at which the news of the merger was announced. In those days, few people in Britain – let alone in expensive Oxford colleges – knew anything about communist political methods, and when the announcement of the merger was made I applauded innocently like everyone else. We had moved on to the next item on the agenda before a vague suspicion prompted me to ask the chairman when we had been consulted about the merger. The reply was friendly but evasive, and I asked another question. Other members joined in, and it soon became clear that the merger was simply a communist takeover, fixed up between the open communists of the October Club and the secret communists of the Labour Club. Three or four of us thereupon decided to oppose the merger. Though we were too late to succeed in this, we resolved to stick together and keep the flag of democratic socialism flying inside the new club, which was now in fact a large and powerful communist-dominated organization.

We called ourselves the Oxford University Democratic Socialist Group, and I was elected the first chairman. We drafted a constitution and issued membership cards, and supported each other at meetings and at elections, wearing a special red-and-white tie to give us courage. This mutual aid was very necessary. It needed a strong nerve to stand up and oppose leftist resolutions at our fervent, crowded meetings.

I believe there were nearly two hundred members of the Communist Party at Oxford at this time, including some of the ablest and most intelligent undergraduates. After the merger, they dominated the Labour Club – whose membership sometimes exceeded 1500 – using techniques that became familiar enough later but frequently caught us off our guard at that time.

Our greatest difficulty was to discover which of our social democratic colleagues were secret communists, and which were not. After a time I began to think I had become good at this, but many years later – long after the war – when I met one of the leading members of our anti-communist group and reminded him of our campaigning, he sheepishly confessed that he had been a communist all along, having joined our group on party instructions. I felt extremely annoyed.

We were also handicapped by the communist practice of rigging elections. A friend who took part in this and who left the Communist Party soon afterwards told me how the system worked. The voting was fair, and so was the counting of the votes: all the communists did was to announce the wrong results. After the count, they would meet to decide 'in an atmosphere of considerable hilarity' whom they would declare elected. A particularly engaging point is that they did not always declare the communist candidates elected. On the contrary, in 1936, after the Communist International had called for a 'united front of all progressive forces against fascism and war', they were so anxious to demonstrate their loyalty to the new tactic that they sometimes declared a non-communist elected when he had been fairly beaten by a communist. Whether my own repeated election to the executive committee was fair or faked I have never been able to discover.

At about this time, I allowed myself to be drawn into an international conference 'of all parties and of none' at Brussels, which had been engineered by a Stalinist front organization. I was trapped by flattery: 'If people like yourself do not come, your point of view will go by default'; 'we strongly disagree with your views, but we must admit

A War of Words

that you put them over well, and we want all points of view represented.' The appeal was plausible and I fell for it. Communist techniques at international conferences were then a comparative novelty and I learned a useful lesson. The Stalinists laid on the trappings of democracy thickly, but they controlled all the key committees, including those that drafted the resolutions, the agenda and the speakers' list. My feeble ingenuous efforts to get some hearing for noncommunist opinions were blandly ignored. In the fervent atmosphere created (one high point was the appearance of a masked figure on the platform – a 'member of the German, anti-Nazi underground') any effective dissent from the Stalinist line was out of the question.

Strangely enough, our bitter struggles did not prevent all factions in the Labour Club at Oxford from uniting effectively on specific campaigns. Sometimes, we would deploy in fleets of buses to London or the Home Counties for a demonstration or a by-election. When an army of hunger marchers descended upon Oxford from south Wales, we organized a reception committee, which found them beds and food. I arranged a meal for a large number of them – south Wales miners – and was rewarded by an invitation to stay with one of the miners in Dowlais. I readily accepted this, and kept in contact with my friendly host for many years.

Labour Club members also dominated the Oxford Union, consistently winning the arguments and debates and getting our own candidates elected to the various offices; in 1937, forgetful of our internal battle, my communists and fellow-travelling colleagues flooded into the polling booths at the Union to elect me as president with a record majority.

The task of democratic socialists in the Labour Club had always been an uphill one, but in 1936 our problems were greatly increased by the Comintern's worldwide 'United Front' campaign, calling for 'the unity of all progressive forces against fascism and war'.

This call made a big impact, not least in Britain, where many members of Labour and Liberal parties, including some leading Labour figures, responded enthusiastically. So did the great majority of student socialists. Though few in number and widely distrusted, the communists were disciplined and extremely active and became the dominant force in the campaign. They used every opportunity to increase their own membership, and to impose their own tactics and slogans.

This situation was unacceptable to many other left-wing opponents of Nazism. These included the Labour leaders, who eventually decreed that unless the University Labour Federation (ULF) (which represented all the university's Labour clubs) expelled its communists, it would be disaffiliated by the Labour Party. A bitter struggle ensued in which I became deeply involved. A leading article in *University Forward*, the ULF's newspaper, stated:

On page three there appears a letter from Comrade Mayhew. Its opening sentence mentions a 'formal declaration of war between the ULF and the Labour Party.' What an irresponsible statement for a leading socialist student to make! The Labour Party has not declared 'war' upon us. And we had no intention of declaring 'war' upon the Labour Party of which we are a loyal part. Every effort must be made to reach an amicable settlement. We must, however, be sure that in our anxiety to remain within the Labour Movement, we do not blind ourselves to what would happen if comrade Mayhew's readiness to expel our communists were to be widely accepted...

To expel the communists would be to lose far more than the communists. It would be to lose hundreds of other good comrades who would leave our Federation in disgust. It would mean the disintegration of the ULF.[3]

My letter had been as follows:

The formal declaration of war between the ULF and the Labour Party surprises no one who really understands these two organizations. The possibility of trouble has been regularly referred to by the democratic socialists, and was mentioned by them at the ULF's Manchester conference.

Only the communists and other members of the 'Unity' brigade steadily took no notice, either failing to foresee it, with their famous lack of political judgement, or else tactfully ignoring it...

The choice before us is between losing our communists as active members and losing the entire goodwill and support of the Labour Party and of the many undergraduates in the University, some of them now members of the ULF, who intend to remain faithful to it. It is a clear choice; and an unimpassioned consideration of the pros and cons can only lead to one answer – that (with the success of university socialism as the criterion) it is far more important to remain on terms with the Labour Party than to keep our communists as active members.

However, the climate of undergraduate opinion was strongly against this. The climax came at a specially summoned conference of all university socialist groups, addressed by the Labour Party's national agent, Mr George Shepherd. The forces of democratic socialism were hopelessly outnumbered, and our little group from Oxford had to do battle with hordes of communists and fellow-travellers virtually alone. The conference ended on a depressing note of farce. Mr Shepherd was stoutly built, and when he finished his long speech on our behalf and sat down, his chair collapsed beneath him. Our enemies cheered and laughed delightedly, and our rout was complete.

Two years later, of course, when the communists were supporting Joseph Stalin's pact with Adolf Hitler and opposing the war, the 'Unity' campaign and the ULF ignominiously collapsed. It was left to the next generation of Oxford undergraduates (which included Roy Jenkins and Tony Crosland) to split the Labour Club and found a socialist organization at the university that made some political sense.

By 1939 I had become a Labour candidate for Parliament and had joined the Territorial Army. From then until the end of the war, I had only one brush with communists. On leave from the British Expeditionary Force in France, I attended the annual general meeting of my constituency party – (South Norfolk). In my absence, the party had moved to the left, influenced by a handful of local communists, who were opposing the war, following the lead of the Soviet Union. One of the resolutions put forward was: 'That the Parliamentary Labour Party should press the Government to take the lead in calling a conference of all European nations at once, with the object of arriving at a basis on which a firm and lasting peace in the interests of the working classes of the world can be established.'

My speech was reported in the *Eastern Daily Press*:

Mr Mayhew opposed the resolution. Familiarity with the weapons of war had brought him to hate war more than ever, he said, but he could see no alternative to standing firm. Calling another conference at this moment would mean calling another Munich conference on a vaster and more tragic scale. It would stop the war, but for how long? Just long enough, he thought, for Hitler to exploit the advantage he would win from us and build a fleet as well – and then war again. . . .

However, despite this plea from its candidate, made personally, in uniform, the party carried this communist-inspired resolution by a majority vote.

In 1945, I won South Norfolk in the Labour landslide victory and became Parliamentary Private Secretary to the Deputy Prime Minister and Leader of the House, Herbert Morrison. In 1946, he arranged for me to represent the Labour Party at the annual conference of the German Social Democratic Party in Bavaria. This was an important assignment. The German social democrats were faced with a fateful decision – whether or not to join the communist-led Socialist Unity Party – and were looking to their much-admired British colleagues for a lead. After consulting the Labour Party's general secretary, Morgan Phillips, I decided, boldly, to urge them in my speeches to break with the communists and strike out on their own. For whatever reason, they decided to do this, and on my return I found I had surprised and angered both left-wing and centrist Labour MPs. They complained, with some justice, that I had had no authority for speaking as I did. However – so Morrison told me – Ernest Bevin, as foreign secretary, was delighted. There was a vacancy for parliamentary secretary at the Foreign Office and Bevin persuaded Attlee to appoint me. My anti-communist campaigning then began in earnest.

Chapter 2
Propaganda and the Workers' Paradise

When I arrived at the Foreign Office in September 1946, Britain was engaged in the cold war single-handedly. The policy of the United States' government, vehemently supported by the US Congress, was to avoid any foreign entanglements. But Britain was deploying 40,000 troops in propping up the Western-orientated Greek government against a formidable Stalin-backed communist insurgency. British servicemen were being killed and our reserves of foreign exchange were draining away.

Through his huge worldwide propaganda machine, Stalin was presenting the confrontation in Greece as the repression of Greek democracy by British imperialism, and this theme was being obligingly echoed in the British Parliament and elsewhere by a sizeable section of the Parliamentary Labour Party. Some of the first parliamentary questions I had to answer dealt with allegations that the government was condoning the persecution of Greek trade unionists.

My diary of 3 June 1947 gives a picture of Bevin's feelings at the time. We were dining at the Chilean embassy:

Polish ambassador sits opposite SS [Secretary of State]. SS embarks on a tremendous argument about Greece – Michawowski replying in spirited fashion. This leads on to a diatribe against Russian policy, and Joe Stalin in particular. Obviously Bevin's remarks were meant to reach Joe and certainly will. He said that peace will never be secure while Russia supports civil war in other countries – in Persia, in Greece. 'The day Russia calls off her bloodhounds in Greece, the peace of that country will be assured.' 'The bandits are using anti-aircraft guns now: bandits don't find them for themselves.' 'The trouble is Stalin. He is an irascible man. It's not [Vyacheslav] Molotov's or [Andrey] Vyshinsky's fault. They don't count. They have not the power. It is Stalin. He is so irascible. You can't deal with men like that. But if affairs like Persia go on, America will lose patience, and then what will happen?'

In the midst of all this, he lets slip an aside to Mrs Noel-Baker (wife of Cabinet minister, and future Nobel peace prizewinner, Philip Noel-Baker) who is sitting between us. 'Of course I am doing all this on purpose', laughing away to himself. But it's not only duty which makes him talk like this – also he wants to get it off his chest to Joe, even at one remove, through the Polish ambassador. He is sincerely bitter, and his personal feelings are all mixed up in it. It's all rather grand and exciting, but also disturbing.

However, help was at hand. A few months before, the British government had informed President Harry Truman that we could no longer sustain our military and economic aid to Greece; and he had responded bravely with the famous 'Truman doctrine': 'It must be the policy of the United States to support free peoples who are resisting attempted subjugation by armed minorities or outside pressures.' By May 1947, Truman had persuaded Congress to authorize $400 million economic aid to Greece and Turkey; and this proved enough to stabilize the regimes there. But Britain had led the way.

Britain was also ahead of the United States in responding to the worldwide Soviet propaganda offensive. At first, Bevin was resistant to the proposal for a counteroffensive. 'The more I see of this, the less I like it' was his scrawled, emphatic minute on a memorandum submitted by senior officials in June 1946. It recommended the launching of a worldwide anti-communist propaganda campaign.

The memorandum was logical and well argued, but also premature, and too negative. At this time, Bevin still hoped for a general settlement with Stalin. Indeed, by the end of the year he seemed quite confident about this. My diary records on 20 December 1946:

I had a long talk (or rather audience) with him. He describes his general views on the UN General Assembly and the future. He is full of repressed optimism and delight and self congratulation, keeping it all under with an effort and talking in terms of the dangers of over-optimism. He said to Molotov on the boat something about the better atmosphere in New York. Molotov replied 'I think we are learning how to cooperate.' Ernie attributes much of the toughness and bitterness of Russian diplomacy to inexperienced personnel. This won't stand though, but it may be a contributory factor.

For myself, I had always been sceptical about a general settlement with Stalin, and this view was strengthened in 1947 by experience of Soviet conduct at United Nations conferences. In March 1947, I wrote home from a conference of the Economic and Social Council.

The proceedings of the Council are the most restful affairs in the world. Not only is it unnecessary to pay any attention to half the speeches – e.g. a self-advertising speech about Peru by the Peruvian – but they all have to be translated at least once, which means that you can read, write or just doze away for fully half the time. But now and again you must look out for yourself, as the Slavs are sometimes apt to spring a fast one. On Friday, for example, I mentioned in the course of a speech that until the Human Rights Commission had framed at least the outline of its Bill of Rights little effective work could be done by the subcommission concerned with seeing that these rights were enjoyed by minorities. The Russian quickly picked this up, misquoting me as saying that I did not consider the subcommission's work important, and explaining that unlike Britain, Russia always had the welfare of the oppressed minorities, native peoples etc. close to her heart. So I was forced to improvise a rapid reply.

The aggressive tactics of Soviet delegates were accompanied by highly disciplined self-isolation.

In October 1947, I attended the General Assembly of the United Nations, with Minister of State Hector McNeil. Hector was the delegation leader. He was almost as young and inexperienced as myself, a Scotsman, a former Beaverbrook journalist, courageous, a great mixer.

Our fellow passengers on the *Queen Elizabeth* included many other delegates bound for the UN Assembly, including a large Soviet party led by Vyshinsky, the notorious prosecuting counsel in Stalin's show

Propaganda and the Workers' Paradise

trials. Hector set out to establish a personal relationship with this repellent man. It was a forlorn hope. He sent a bottle of Scotch and a friendly note to Vyshinsky's cabin, but there was no acknowledgement. He then sent some flowers to the cabin of Vyshinsky's daughter, but with no better result.

On board ship, it is difficult to avoid all contacts with fellow passengers, but the Soviet delegates' efforts to achieve this were entirely successful. For most delegates, meal times in the dining saloon were diplomatic occasions – opportunities for meeting one's opposite numbers and breaking barriers. But Vyshinsky ate in his cabin, presumably with his daughter, while the rest of the Soviet delegates would appear punctually, all together, at the entrance to the dining saloon, thread their way between the tables and disappear into a private room. After an appropriate interval, they would then reappear, again all together, and make their retreat, speaking to no one on the way.

This self-isolation was a fair warning of the bitter hostility the Soviet delegates were to display towards non-communist delegates in New York. However, Hector had assigned me to Committee 2 of the UN Assembly, dealing with economic affairs, and here the Soviet representative, Amazap Arutiunian, was unusual in several respects. He was not a Russian but an Armenian, and was witty, inquisitive and likeable. I set out to persuade him to have lunch with me alone, and eventually, after many attempts, succeeded. Absurd though it sounds today, this was a diplomatic breakthrough, which I reported to the Foreign Office.

His conversation was discreet but lively and gave me some insight into his thought processes. He took the straight Stalinist line on everything, and evidently believed it all. Taken by themselves, his facts were usually correct, but his Marxist thought processes led him to assemble them into unreal patterns, producing over-simple conclusions. Since there were conditions attached to our loan from the USA, Britain was an economic vassal of the USA. Since British newspapers were owned by capitalists, there was no freedom of the press. Our withdrawal from empire was simply a new form of colonialism.

However, Marxism was still plausible at that time. It offered a single, easily understood method of analysis, and an explanation of the errors of apparently intelligent bourgeois intellectuals.

A War of Words

In 1947, unchallenged by Western governments, Stalin's worldwide campaign of subversion and propaganda was at its most effective. Orchestrated from Moscow, or indirectly through the Cominform, scores of communist and communist-front organizations maintained a relentless war against Western governments and institutions. The Soviet Union was presented as the exact antithesis of the West, that is, as the true enemy of fascism, the champion of colonial peoples against imperialism, the ally of all peace-loving people and the shining example of a workers' state in which capitalism had been abolished and where the workers prospered and were free.

To this flood of propaganda, the Western countries made no organized response at all. The convention among Western delegates was not to reply to Soviet diatribes but simply to deplore the abuse of UN meetings for propaganda purposes and to urge respect for the agenda. After a short experience at the UN, I came to the conclusion that this policy was wrong. Soviet propaganda was having an impact, especially in the Third World, and needed to be answered; and if the answer was to be effective, it must go beyond self-defence and carry the propaganda war into the enemy's camp. We needed, urgently, a propaganda apparatus of our own.

I also felt that social-democratic Britain was better placed than capitalist America to take the lead; and also that a British anti-communist propaganda campaign would be anathema to much of the Labour Party, and would have to be organized discreetly.

On my way home on the *Queen Elizabeth*, unaware of the similar initiative taken unsuccessfully by officials 18 months earlier, I wrote Bevin a long memorandum urging that the time had come for a change of policy towards the Soviet Union.

I argued that the Soviet government simply regarded the United Nations as a useful instrument of political warfare: there was in practice no effective cooperation between East and West through the United Nations machinery. If the United Nations did not exist, the way would be clearer for closer cooperation between the countries of Western Europe, as fear of 'bypassing the United Nations' still exercised a restraining influence. Nevertheless, we should oppose American suggestions that the Soviet Union should be manoeuvred out of the UN: this would leave our left flank open, in the long years ahead, to the false but dangerous accusation of having repelled the Soviet Union while she was still willing to cooperate. On the other hand, we should not sacrifice any chance of greater cooperation with and integration of Western Europe through inhibitions about 'bypassing the UN'. After November, if the Council of Foreign Ministers failed, we should launch a sustained worldwide anti-communist propaganda offensive. This would stress the weakness of communism, not its strength, revealing Russia as a poor, backward, devastated country with ridiculous pretensions of being a 'liberator' and 'the wave of the future'. It would sell social democracy strongly and avoid opposing communism as a defender of the 'status quo'. It would be truthful, well documented and closely argued, and should be designed for journalists, public speakers, trade unionists, and political organizers at home and abroad who were up against communist opposition.[1]

Bevin seemed disposed to agree with the memorandum, and told me to discuss it with senior officials and to prepare a paper suitable for presentation to Attlee. A meeting was duly held on 18 November, attended by Sir Orme Sargent, the permanent under-secretary, Mr Ivone Kirkpatrick, assistant under-secretary and Mr C. F. A. Warner, head of the Information Department. The meeting quickly agreed on the need to launch a counteroffensive. However, the officials were silent about my proposal that our campaign should stress the merits of social democracy and should criticize the evils of capitalism along with those of communism.

I now realize that, more experienced than myself, these officials realized that this idea was impracticable, but did not wish to rock the boat at that stage. My support for it was naive but honest, and I felt that my proposal would appeal to Bevin and Attlee. Moreover, as parliamentary under-secretary, I was acutely aware that, in addition to the score or so of communists and fellow-travellers, a substantial further section of the Parliamentary Party, led by Dick Crossman and Michael Foot, was already strongly critical of the government for its coolness towards the Soviet Union and relative friendliness with the United States. If the proposed change of policy of the government became known – and leaks seemed to be inevitable – I felt that it could be seriously undermined by hostile speeches in parliament from Dick Crossman and others.

A War of Words

I also found myself at odds with the officials as to the principal line of attack of our propaganda campaign. While they thought that dictatorship should be the principal object of attack, my own view was that for the masses of people in Europe and the Third World at that time, living standards were still more important. Eventually, we reached a compromise on this without much difficulty.

The Council of Foreign Ministers (CFM) was now about to meet in London in a final attempt to reach an East/West agreement on the future of Germany. I gave an impression of the conference in a letter to my family:

Now and again I go to Lancaster House for the meetings, usually sitting on the left of the rest of our delegation, next to Marshal Sokolovsky, Vyshinsky and Molotov. Sitting next to Molotov, you would think, at this crucial conference in the world's history, would be the greatest thrill imaginable. How wrong. After the first five minutes it's just excruciatingly boring. The great men wrangle away interminably, usually on procedure, and everything they say has to be translated twice. The windows of the small room are tiny, and the air gets hotter and hotter and thicker and thicker, and you long for 6.30, when everyone beats it to the bar...

Molotov and Vyshinsky know my name and face now, and we exchange a few words. I told Molotov that part of my job was reindoctrinating wayward Labour MPs who went to Russia to see him during Parliamentary recesses. He emitted a (for him) hearty laugh, and said he was sure that kept me busy.... It's exciting enough meeting these world figures at any time; but when you find three or four of them in your queue at the cloakroom the thing becomes a kind of fantasy.

My diary for 13 December records:

The truth is that EB is not doing well at the CFM. There is a lack of leadership, initiative and even clear thinking in our delegation. Ernest knows he's below par. He's not at all fit physically.... Ernest keeps saying 'Will anyone tell me what to do next?' at the delegation meeting. He told me yesterday he just had no idea of Molotov's mind and intentions – whether or not he intended agreement after this initial fighting.... No one in the delegation puts the connected, logical case, and no one is constructive or sounds confident.

21 December:

Well, the CFM's over. We may still get an agreement on Austria but otherwise the conference has been a complete failure. Always knew it would be. Ernest was wrong to expect anything, but he was right as a politician not to give up trying too soon. Or perhaps he never really hoped for anything? No, I don't think that. He had a feeling right up to the last moment that Molotov might suddenly come clean.

Finally despairing of the Russians, Bevin approved my paper and told me to send a copy to Attlee. In due course, it came back with a note expressing 'general agreement' and bidding me to Chequers to discuss it. My diary of 27 December notes:

Went down to Chequers. ... He has no criticism to make of my paper at all, from what I can see, he adds a few suggestions of his own. He thinks we should stress that throughout history Russia's strength has always been overestimated (don't agree – Hitler! – but didn't say so). In general I should say he's more ready for a lead on the ideological front than Ernest is. At the end of our talk (which rambled on for the best part of an hour) he agrees that I should draft a Cabinet paper for next week's meeting, and meanwhile may make small administrative arrangements in anticipation.

3 January:

Yesterday Attlee held me back after a meeting of the defence committee to show me his draft broadcast in the political debate series of the BBC. It is strongly 'Third Force' in flavour, hits out against Russia and is ruder to the USA than even I think wise. He readily agrees that I should take it away and mess it about. This I do, and take the opportunity of inserting 'The history of Soviet Russia provides us with a warning, a warning that without political freedom collectivism can quickly go astray and lead to new forms of injustice and oppression. For political freedom is not merely *a noble thing in itself, essential for the full development of human personality – it is also a means of achieving economic rights and social justice, and for preserving these things when they had been won. Where there is no political freedom privilege and injustice creep back. In communist Russia 'privilege for the few' is a growing phenomenon and the gap between the highest and the lowest incomes is constantly widening. Soviet communism pursues a policy which threatens with a new form of imperialism – ideological, economic and strategic – the welfare and way of life of the other countries of Europe.'*

Though mild enough by later standards, this criticism of the Soviet Union broke new ground and was a useful send-off to our propaganda campaign.

The paper 'Future Foreign Publicity Policy' did not have an easy ride in Cabinet.[2] Although the minutes of Cabinet meetings do not normally attribute particular statements to particular ministers, it must surely have been Aneurin Bevan who declared:

It was important that in the execution of the policy outlined too much emphasis should not be laid on its anti-Soviet aspect. A policy which gained unanimous support of the press and public of the right would fail to rally the socialist forces in Western Europe and would make it more difficult to foster cultural and trade relations with Eastern European countries which, though dominated politically by communists, still have a Western outlook. The danger of pursuing a policy which concentrated on opposition to the Soviet government was illustrated by events in Greece.

Bevin fought back warmly and at length. It would be impossible for him, he said, to give an effective lead without being critical of Soviet policy, but it was his intention to concentrate mainly on the positive and constructive side of his proposals. The most effective method of countering Soviet propaganda was to provide specific information refuting the misrepresentations made by the Soviet government. The Prime Minister's recent broadcast illustrated how this could be combined with encouragement of socialist principles. Eventually, the Cabinet, 'subject to the points made in discussion', endorsed the policy outlined in the paper.

Propaganda and the Workers' Paradise

Back in the Foreign Office, a number of administrative decisions were quickly taken. We were heartened by the sure knowledge that Ernest Bevin would not wish us to take the slightest notice of any points made in discussion by Aneurin Bevan. He decided to create a new department in the Foreign Office and call it the 'Information Research Department' (IRD). No attempt would be made to conceal its existence, or the names of its staff, but to protect it from possible political attacks from the left, the fact that its specific role was anti-communist propaganda would be kept secret.

When I left the Foreign Office (having lost my seat in the 1950 general election) I took with me a few personal papers relating to IRD. Unaccountably, the rest of the papers were kept under wraps by the Foreign Office. But then, in 1993, irritated by some hostile 'leaks' about the IRD in the United States, I began pressing the government to release these papers, and in due course the then foreign secretary, Douglas Hurd, agreed. In 1995, the first batches of archives were released.

I found it unnerving to be suddenly confronted with the minutes and memoranda I had written 50 years before. There they were, long forgotten but instantly recognizable. I soon saw that I had taken rather more wrong decisions and rather fewer right ones than I had remembered; also that once the IRD had been launched, my contribution to its development had been limited. There had been good reasons for this: I was often abroad at that time, and my duties included understudying Bevin over the whole field of his activities – in Parliament, in the Foreign Office, even, occasionally, in the Cabinet. Supervising anti-communist propaganda was only one of my many responsibilities. It was as though I had launched a ship, and then watched it slowly rolling away from me down the slipway, to become accessible thereafter only by radio, and only on special occasions.

The Foreign Office machine went into action quickly and efficiently. On 25 February, Orme Sargent circularized all our overseas missions to inform them of the new policy, emphasizing that its implementation was the task of the whole mission and not merely of their information officers.

Kirkpatrick, who had masterminded the earlier submission to Bevin for a counteroffensive, quickly laid down an establishment for the IRD and began recruiting staff. Many recruits were immigrants from Iron Curtain countries, often journalists and writers. Others came from the ranks of the government's regional information units, which were being slimmed down. An able and energetic officer, Mr (later Sir) Ralph Murray, was appointed the IRD's first director. Another source of strength to the IRD, then and later, was Mr Norman Reddaway, whom I had seized, with some difficulty, from the German department to be my private secretary. During the war we had served in the same unit in North Africa. Exceptionally inventive and resourceful, Reddaway became the IRD's deputy director in 1955, ending a distinguished career as ambassador in Warsaw.

I now made an extraordinary mistake. One day, Hector McNeil came into my room, congratulated me on the progress the IRD was making, and said he had someone available who was uniquely qualified for IRD work. I replied that I was now only taking people with exceptional knowledge of Soviet communism. Who was this candidate? 'My personal assistant, Guy Burgess. Just your man.'

I did not feel enthusiastic about this, having come across Burgess in Hector's outer office. Often enough he would be leaning against the mantelpiece with an unattended cigarette dangling from his lips, apparently quite idle. However, I interviewed him. Not unnaturally, he showed a dazzling insight into communist methods of subversion and propaganda, and I readily took him on. Fortunately, a few months later, Norman Reddaway warned me to look at Burgess's work. I made some inquiries and dismissed him from the IRD, minuting on his file 'Burgess is dirty, drunken and idle.' However, it never occurred to me that he was also a Soviet agent. Nor did this occur to anyone else in the Foreign Office, or in MI5. After a short period, Burgess was appointed to the Far East Department, and afterwards to the Washington embassy, where he continued his work for the Russians in close contact with Philby.

At one time I thought that the KGB must have instructed Burgess to join the IRD. I now think that the explanation is more prosaic – that Hector seized the opportunity of IRD's formation to get rid of him from his private office.

Ironically, I was being attacked at this time by left-wing MPs as a 'McCarthyite'. At a meeting of the Parliamentary Labour Party, a

Clydeside MP, Emrys Hughes, declared amid applause: 'The trouble with Chris Mayhew is that he sees communists under every bed.'

No sooner had the IRD been established than difficulties emerged over projecting the positive side of its message. As a number of overseas missions were quick to point out, the concepts of social democracy and the 'third force' had little or no meaning in their countries, while criticism of capitalism would be seen as interference in domestic politics. My view that the IRD should have a positive as well as a negative message had probably helped to recommend it to Bevin, Attlee and the Cabinet, and to make it less vulnerable to possible attack from the left. But I could not contest these powerful arguments and conceded that in most countries the dual task was simply not practicable.

Fortunately, the opinions of ministers and Labour MPs were changing rapidly at this time. A few weeks after the launching of the IRD, the communist coup in Czechoslovakia produced a rapid and salutary decline in Stalinist illusions in the Parliamentary Labour Party, and reduced the risk of left-wing opposition to the government's new policy.

Bevin's position in the Party was further strengthened by his famous speech in the Commons on 22 January 1948, launching the concept of West European unity. This was welcomed by the great majority of Labour MPs, including the Foot/Crossman group.

I had played some part in drafting this speech. In January 1948, a Cabinet paper, called 'The First Aim of British Foreign Policy', had been presented by Bevin to the Cabinet, where it was approved. It urged the need for a defence union of the Western European countries.

Bevin had spent the weekend before the debate on the Isle of Wight, struggling long hours with his speech. A copy of his draft reached me on the evening before the debate. It was of enormous length and, apart from a long passage about lifting the ban on foreign travel, said nothing new. The idea of bringing the Western European countries together received no mention at all.

Bevin's standing in Parliament was not high at this time, and I was afraid that this speech would do him serious damage. So I went to the office early the next morning and assembled the key passages from his Cabinet paper into a stirring declaration of faith in Western unity, coupled with a demand for a defence union of the European countries.

A War of Words

After hastily clearing this with the permanent under-secretary, then Sir Ivone Kirkpatrick, I burst into Bevin's harassed presence. Surrounded on all sides by bits of the first draft of his speech, he took my paper cheerfully enough and began reading it in his usual slow manner. After a time, he said 'This is a good turn you done, Chris,' and when he had finished reading it, he paused, grunting and wheezing in his familiar way. Finally, he said, with a shade of doubt in his voice, 'It's a tremendous declaration.'

A few hours later he said it all in his speech, with great conviction, to the applause not only of the Commons but virtually the whole Western world.

Sooner or later, I have no doubt, Bevin would have made this declaration anyhow, and would doubtless then have been careful to consult and inform friendly governments beforehand. As it was, not only our friends abroad but our own embassies were taken completely by surprise, and the office was flooded with requests for further information. I sent Bevin a rather defensive note the next day urging him to set up a special working party to plan the next steps.

Nevertheless, this speech had a profound effect. In due course, the Western European Union was formed, and afterwards NATO, and later, with the failure of the blockade of Berlin, the balance of power slowly swung against Stalin. One day Bevin said to me, with somewhat vindictive gusto, that at last he had some cards to play against Molotov. He had waited three years, three years of humiliation, but Molotov would have to listen to him now.

Meantime, the IRD was quickly getting into its stride. An immediate task was to try to help the hard-pressed anti-communist forces in the critical Italian general election of April 1948. By a special effort, the IRD managed to make some of its early output available to selected journalists, candidates and party organizers.

The IRD's basic method of operation was to disseminate well-researched facts about Soviet communism to our missions and information services abroad. But equally important was the provision of this material to leading British and foreign journalists and broadcasters. IRD papers were based on research of the highest quality, which drew on secret service information as well as material gathered openly from overseas missions. Exaggeration, distortion and disinformation were unnecessary and were firmly ruled out: the facts about Stalinism spoke for themselves.

This service was often greatly valued by those publicists selected to receive it. They were told as little as possible about the IRD. Material would be sent to their homes under plain cover. They were to be told that the documents were not official policy and should not be attributed to HMG, but that they had been prepared for members of the diplomatic service in the Foreign Office. The official 'caveat' read:

The attached material on ... is for the use of His Majesty's missions, and information officers in particular.

The information contained in this paper is, so far as is possible to ascertain, factual and objective. The paper may therefore be used freely, as a reference paper, but neither copies of it nor material contained in it should be distributed officially without the sanction of the head of Mission. It and all the material in the paper, however, may be distributed unofficially in whatever quarters seem useful so long as it can be assured that there will be no public attribution of the material or of the paper to an official British source.

This careful formula, by declaring that the information was for official use, gave it added credibility: at the same time it could, in an emergency, be defended in Parliament.

The recipients included publicists of many different shades of political opinion and some of the most respected writers on foreign affairs. When the IRD was closed in 1977, its list of contacts included journalists working for the *Sunday Times*, *Sunday Telegraph*, the *Observer*, *Sunday Mirror*, *News of the World*, the *Daily Mail*, *Daily Telegraph*, the *Guardian*, *The Times*, *Financial Times*, *Soviet Analyst* and the *Economist*. At one time the *Economist's* 'Confidential Report' drew an average of 50 per cent of its material from the IRD. This report was avidly read by London diplomats and no doubt provided them with material for their dispatches home.

The attitudes of journalists towards IRD material varied considerably. Many realized that they were being fed a British viewpoint and used IRD material with extreme caution, if at all. Some were well aware of its anti-communist/pro-British nature and supported this wholeheartedly for patriotic motives. Others, like William Forrest, foreign correspondent at the News Chronicle, were grateful for the time and effort saved by the research and factual information provided, finding the service of great value and feeling free to select the facts required for their particular needs. Although William Forrest, not inaccurately, thought that the material 'was produced by the FO backroom boys', he was unaware that it was produced by a special propaganda department.

This service to journalists was not the full extent of the IRD's press operations. We also made arrangements with several British newspapers, on payment of a fee, to allow them to select, reprint and distribute suitable articles for republication abroad. The *Observer*, *The Times* and the *Sunday Times* were all involved in this way. Only the author and publication would be acknowledged in the reprint and not the official source. It was also a condition of the agreement that the articles could not in any way be altered. In effect, this arrangement meant that views critical of Soviet communism were being disseminated abroad, apparently from the British press in a straightforward way.

In the first three months of the IRD's existence, briefs were prepared and circulated on the real conditions in Soviet Russia (11 March); conditions in the communist-dominated states of eastern Europe (12 March); Poland as an example of how communism gains and consolidates control in a state (18 March); equality and class distinction in the Soviet Union (24 March); labour and trade unions in the Soviet Union (7 April); the communization of justice in eastern Europe (10 April); communism and the freedom of the press (10 April); the facts of Soviet expansionism (25 May) and peasant collectivization (25 May).

The recipients included – besides our missions abroad and journalists – selected ministers, MPs, trade union leaders, the international department of the Labour Party, the BBC World Service and the foreign offices of friendly countries.

In April 1949, the first edition of *Points at Issue* was printed. This was a small booklet, the size of a pocket diary, which condensed all the basic propaganda points being stressed by the IRD. I suggested to Bevin that we should not deal with this as a routine matter but publish it on a big scale in different languages. However, sponsorship presented a problem, and it was finally decided to give it 'the widest circulation, short of actual publication, through normal channels'. The handbook proved popular and, by the end of 1949, some 8000 copies had already been distributed.

After a number of false starts, the IRD eventually settled on a practical and successful system for publishing and distributing books and booklets. It started using a small publishing company, Ampersand Ltd, which published IRD material for 20 years. A director of Ampersand, Stephen Watts, created and edited a series of more than 100 volumes of 'Background Books'. The IRD paid for the books by buying copies of the titles it wanted, and then distributed them free of charge to British embassies, schools and colleges around the world.

The first Background Book, *What is Communism?* by an anonymous 'student of affairs', was translated into German, Arabic, Portuguese and Greek. When I later became a backbencher, I wrote a Background Book, *What is Titoism?*, in which I was much helped by my wife Ciccly, who had served as a junior diplomat in the British embassy in Belgrade at the time of the Marshal Tito/Joseph Stalin split.

Other authors of Background Books, or contributors to them, included Bertrand Russell, Robert Conquest, Vic Feather, Brian Crozier, Lord Dacre (then Hugh Trevor-Roper) and Hugh Seton Watson.

Critical to the IRD's success was its relationship with the BBC. This raised particularly delicate problems. Any attempt to influence the home services was obviously out of the question: but would it be right to offer IRD material to the external services, which were funded by the Foreign Office vote? These services had established a reputation for reliability, accuracy and quality that had not been tarnished by any dissemination of false material during the war years. Bevin was strongly opposed to suggestions that the government's relationship with the BBC on overseas broadcasts should be changed, or that the BBC should be required to accept definite official direction on the content of its broadcasts. He said 'I should not be in favour of this. It would raise very serious issues here and might well diminish the influence and reputation in foreign countries of the BBC's broadcasts.'

Eventually, the White Paper on broadcasting published in July 1948 declared 'The Corporation should remain independent in the preparation of programmes for overseas audiences, though it should obtain from Government departments concerned such information about conditions in those countries and the polices of His Majesty's Government toward them, and will permit it to plan its programmes in the national interest.'

The Director General of the BBC, Sir Ian Jacob, was a member of the Foreign Office's Russia Committee, and was discreet and cooperative. He agreed that a supply of IRD briefs should be laid on for the controller of the overseas services and the editor of the European Service. Anatole Goldberg, chief commentator for the eastern European services of the BBC, knew about the IRD from the start. He recalled that his contacts with the department were personal and that he maintained very good relationships with various IRD representatives. He found the department helpful in that it gave 'documentary facts, and the government's view on a particular issue – it was useful with sensible people'. The value of the material obtained from the IRD was that it 'supplemented in more detailed form, the information obtained by the diplomatic correspondent from the News Desk at the Foreign Office'.[3] Dr George Urban was a member of the BBC European Service from late 1947 to 1960. He recalls: 'The Foreign Office ran in those days (albeit with a somewhat guilty conscience and with minimum publicity) a very effective information and research department (IRD) which did stirring work in countering communist disinformation, supporting publications deemed tactically useful, supplying the BBC, too, with confidential material, at a time when the USSR and Eastern Europe were almost hermetically sealed off.'[4] In practice, despite jamming, much anti-communist propaganda was broadcast to Iron Curtain countries, though the principle was strictly observed that there should be no incitement to subversive activities where the government was in no position to provide assistance to overthrowing their regimes.

According to Sir Hugh Greene, head of the eastern European services in 1949/50, the IRD was known to those broadcasting to the communist world as an anti-communist department for propaganda. Its main function, as he recalled, was: 'The supply of factual information ... the type of material was not news in the strictest sense but useful factual information for the occasional commentary.' Sir Hugh did not find the department intrusive in any way: 'it was never in the forefront of one's mind, just another source of factual information from which one could select. The BBC always had complete editorial authority – the freedom to take or leave IRD material, and that's what we did. We used the research facts as necessary.' Sir Hugh felt that a department supplying information on Russia was needed at that time: 'if the IRD had not been formed, then some other FO department would have been necessary.'[5]

One of the IRD's earliest tasks was to formulate a policy for propaganda to, and about, the British colonies. Anti-colonial propaganda was a major feature of the Soviet ideological challenge, and had been markedly successful over the years in painting a picture of Britain as 'reactionary' and the Soviet Union as 'progressive' in the treatment of 'backward peoples'. This view was widely accepted in the United States, and made an impact even in Britain itself.

Drafting a policy directive called for cooperation between the Foreign Office, the Commonwealth Relations Office and the Colonial Office. I shared this task with my opposite numbers, Patrick Gordon Walker for the Commonwealth and David Rees-Williams (later Lord Ogmore) for the Colonies. Gordon Walker (who was later for a few months foreign secretary in the first Wilson government) had been my tutor in modern history at Oxford, where we had struggled together, master and pupil, against the assaults on the Labour Party from the communist left. It was pleasant now to resume hostilities against communism as government ministers. Our views on colonial propaganda coincided, while differing from those of the Colonial Office. We felt it would be a serious error to get drawn into dispute with the Soviet Union about the merits or demerits of British colonialism. This was the ground of the Russians' choosing, where we were vulnerable. As one Foreign Office adviser, John Pilcher, later our ambassador in Peking, put it to me at the time:

It is very difficult for us to push pro-colonial or pro-commonwealth stuff in Asia. ... Most damning of all is the stupid racial superiority current in many colonies and its application by innumerable memsahibs, which does us more harm than major political blunders. ... I think that we should ask the Colonial Office to conduct very serious propaganda, at least in Malaya and Hong Kong, against prevalent and damaging racial snobbery.

Gordon Walker and I agreed that the only effective argument in defence of the colonial empire was that it was, by mutual agreement, being steadily dissolved, and that the best way of meeting Soviet propaganda was by attacking Soviet colonialism in eastern Europe and, to a lesser extent, in the old tsarist colonies within its frontiers. Murray himself believed priority should go to the second target, and there was plainly a strong case to be made here: the 'autonomy' of the so-called 'autonomous republics' was plainly a façade, and religion, local customs and traditions were brutally suppressed. On the other hand, advances were undoubtedly being made there in education and living standards and, in vivid contrast with British colonies, there was no colour bar.

Disagreements with the Colonial Office caused some delay in reaching our propaganda directive. But eventually agreement was reached and embodied in a circular issued on 12 August 1948.[6]

From the start, our new propaganda policy had been made known to the United States government by our Washington embassy. Warner was always anxious that the IRD's activities should not be slowed down or complicated by the need to consult other governments, and it was agreed that cooperation between ourselves and the Americans should be confined to an exchange of information. In fact, they were well behind us in the organization of anti-communist propaganda, and, in addition, their priorities were different from our own: they wished to concentrate on the satellite countries, mainly through broadcasting, while our activities took many forms and covered most of the world.

I did not altogether agree with Warner about cooperation with friendly governments. The dangers of consultation were clear enough, but I wrote – I now think wrongly:

I feel that the major danger is not that we might have our hands tied too much by working in cooperation, but that, working in isolation, we should fail to make our influence sufficiently felt in building up a concerted counteroffensive. Other countries need our moral encouragement in the feeble efforts most of them put up to defend themselves against communist political warfare.

I had been disappointed earlier, when, on Bevin's recommendation, in line with Warner's views, the Brussels Treaty governments had agreed to exchange information but to 'pursue individual information policies'. By mid-1949, the IRD had sent some 28 research briefs to our Brussels Treaty allies, but the results, though not negligible, had been limited. The Belgian reaction had been good – following the remarks by the foreign minister, Monsieur Spaak, at a ministerial meeting in 1949 that the British government disposed of a mass of information about conditions of life in the Soviet Union and the satellite countries, which he himself did not possess. If it could be made available to him by the British government it would save him the trouble and expense of setting up a parallel Belgian organization to do the same work as that which was being done in Great Britain.

Early in 1949, ever hopeful, I suggested to Bevin that when the Atlantic Pact was formed we should take a strong lead in encouraging its members to cooperate in combating communist propaganda; and when the pact was ratified Gladwyn Jebb (later Lord Gladwyn) submitted a detailed proposal to establish a NATO subcommittee for this purpose. However, Bevin was not persuaded. He minuted: 'I am not enthusiastic for more machinery.' I now think he was right: we were so much better placed than other countries to conduct the anti-communist propaganda campaign, and so far ahead of them, that it was best to forge ahead on our own.

There was much anxiety at that time about the possible impact of Stalinism in the newly emerging Commonwealth countries, especially in India and Pakistan. It is difficult now to realize how acute the problem seemed to be at the time. There were communist parties in most of the countries, putting out lively anti-colonial and anti-British propaganda based on a nationalist appeal. It seemed inconceivable that the Russians wouldn't get their hands on some part of our liberated empire. Given their growing success in winning power in eastern Europe, why not also in these unstable, inexperienced, weak, newly independent countries?

A major problem so far as India was concerned was the non-aligned attitude of the Indian government. It was decided that Sir Archibald Nye, our high commissioner in New Delhi, should sound Jawaharlal Nehru out informally about whether he would be interested in exchanging information on communism. In contrast with his previous negative stance on the subject, Nehru seemed interested, expressing himself willing for such an exchange of information. Material from our side was distinct from that utilized in the secret propaganda programme. Instead, it was more general information derived from diplomatic and intelligence sources. It was recognized that this might well prove to be a one-way street, but the high commissioner was more interested in the change of Nehru's attitude towards communism than in the substance of information to be exchanged. For, in effect, this gave the green light for IRD activity in India. If Nehru's reaction had been unfavourable, then our later decision to proceed with a secret anti-communist information programme would have been far more difficult.

There was no problem about supplying material to Pakistan: the authorities there took the initiative and asked for it. In June 1949, a report from Karachi stated 'The High Commissioner is delighted both with the material you are now supplying and also the volume that is being published in the English and vernacular press ... as long as the existing standard of material is maintained we will be able to keep up our existing record of 100 per cent publication of everything issued.'

In Ceylon, the high commission laid on a supply of material after a personal approach to the prime minister.

Communist insurgency in Southeast Asia presented a special problem. In the autumn of 1948, Nehru and Liaquat Ali, the prime minister of Pakistan, both suggested privately that we should stress the theme of Soviet imperialism in the region. At the suggestion of Malcolm McDonald, high commissioner in Southeast Asia, a regional information office was set up in Singapore, which translated and disseminated IRD material to India, Pakistan and throughout Southeast Asia.

Once IRD had been launched and its overall message and priorities settled, my personal involvement in it diminished. However, as a frequent delegate to the United Nations, I was well placed to use its material there to put up some resistance to Soviet propaganda.

Until that time, our delegates' instructions at the United Nations were to keep our speeches and lobbying relevant to the agenda and not to waste time trying to answer Soviet propaganda. This was the practice of all Western delegates, not least the Americans. I remember Mrs Roosevelt's response to a lengthy Soviet tirade against American imperialism. She simply said that she felt sure the Soviet delegate felt much better now he'd got all that off his chest – could we now address ourselves to the agenda? This was typical of Western practice at that time, and for a sophisticated Western audience it might well have been appropriate. But not all UN delegates were sophisticated or Western: nor was the world's press. It seemed to them a sign of weakness and lack of conviction that the stream of anti-British and anti-American propaganda should go unanswered.

In the belief that the best form of defence would be attack, I asked the IRD to produce briefs on issues where Soviet communism was most vulnerable – slave labour, deportations, human rights abuses and imperialism in eastern Europe. The occasion for delivering this material had to be carefully chosen. While some UN delegates would welcome a spirited Western counterattack to Soviet propaganda, others, especially from the Third World, disliked having the conference agenda hijacked in this way. It was therefore wise to avoid initiating confrontation oneself. Instead, armed with my IRD briefs, I would wait patiently for a Soviet delegate to attack some shortcoming of the United Kingdom or the capitalist West before intervening and answering back. Thus, all my propaganda speeches took the form of replies to Soviet attacks, accompanied by apologies for speaking frankly and for prolonging the proceedings of the conference.[7]

Even so, there was some resistance to my interventions, even within the UK delegation. For example, Mr Grantley Adams, prime minister of Barbados, and a much-valued member of our delegation, objected that it would be better to let Soviet propaganda go unanswered than, in effect, to stultify the positive work of the United Nations.[8] However, the balance of opinion in the delegation was on my side, and I was not discouraged. Moreover, it soon emerged that when Soviet delegates attacked the exploitation of labour in capitalist countries, or the lack of human rights in British colonies, the IRD's brief on Soviet slave labour, what Alexander Solzhenitsyn later called the Gulag, and on Soviet exploitation of eastern Europe, made possible some devastating replies.

The delegates from the communist countries – the Soviet Union, the Ukraine and Belorussia – would object vociferously that there was not a word of truth in what I had said. But IRD research, including many quotations from official Soviet documents and statistics, and many eye-witness reports, was irrefutable. Indeed, with hindsight, it is now clear that at that time we actually understated the scale and horror of the camps and deportations – for example, of Estonians to central Asia.

On 23 October, in a review of the 1948 General Assembly, the UN correspondent for the *New York Times* wrote:

Until this session the Soviet bloc has had things very much their own way in their propaganda. That is not the case any longer. Repeatedly, western spokesmen in committee after committee have hauled the communists over the coals and have fired very effective broadsides through their defences.

Most effective speakers have been the British. The other day Christopher Mayhew answered Russian pretences of social and political freedoms by one of the most scathing factual analyses of Russian labour practices, concentration camps and political punishment ever heard in the United Nations or elsewhere. He cited chapter and verse using official Russian documents and statistics to shatter Russian pretences.

The Soviet delegates were undoubtedly shaken by our onslaught, and in the spring of 1949, before the opening of a session of the UN Social and Economic Council, the leading Soviet delegate, who was again Arutiunian, suggested to me that the conference would be more likely to proceed smoothly if I withdrew an item I had placed on the agenda relating to forced labour. I replied that proceedings would also be helped if the Soviet Union removed its item on the alleged repression of trade unions in Greece and similar provocative subjects. Without much difficulty, we did a deal. With hindsight, I now think I was too generous: but this evidence of the impact of our counteroffensive was encouraging.

Though we never quite trusted each other, Arutiunian and I got on well enough together. Since delegations were placed in alphabetical order – the USSR next to the UK – we sat next to each other for hour after hour of seemingly interminable debates, exchanging cigarettes and expressions of boredom. He had met my future wife, then Cicely Ludlam, a member of the British delegation, and in the course of a session of the Economic and Social Council, when our engagement had been announced in the *Geneva Gazette*, he asked for the floor and declared, amid applause, that the United Kingdom delegate had at last made a proposal for which he could vote, and that he would do so with both my hands.

On another occasion, at a time when Britain had no unemployment problem, and was disarming, Arutiunian made a speech criticizing the British government for attempting to solve its unemployment problem by rearming. When he finished, I asked him with a smile to look me in the eye and tell me he believed a word of it. He replied 'Take off your spectacles first!'

Nevertheless, Arutiunian was in fact a convinced Marxist, and loyal to the Soviet Union – as well as to Armenia – and our occasional private arguments got nowhere. When I wrote him a long personal letter about our political differences, he did not reply.[9] I wondered a good deal about the conditions in which he was working, in particular about the contrast between his speeches eulogizing the freedoms enjoyed in communist countries and the official regimentation of his private life. A few years later, I wrote a television play on this theme, which was broadcast with some success by the BBC and by CBS in the United States (see Chapter 3).

Even without the close attention of their KGB minders, the Soviet delegates were bound to have a hard time at the United Nations. Speaking for the whole communist world, they must have found life extremely stressful. They suffered the further handicap of living and working in the United States. Publicity attended them everywhere, and media representatives were sometimes ill-mannered and tendentious. Admittedly, the Soviet delegates had one great advantage over the rest of us: they were not exposed to public criticism at home; but they deserve credit for their audacity and resoluteness. At a typical UN conference, hundreds of resolutions and amendments would be tabled by non-communist delegates. Very few of them would fail to be met with prepared counter-arguments from Soviet delegates. Now and again, inevitably, they slipped up badly. I remember a Soviet delegate proposing a motion attacking speculators and profiteers in the United States who, he claimed, had forced up the price of American wheat to extortionate levels. He had overlooked the fact, which was pointed out to me by an alert adviser, that at that time Britain was paying a still

A War of Words

higher price for Soviet wheat under the Anglo-Soviet Trade Treaty. When I drew attention to this, the conference was much amused, and the Soviet delegate beat a hasty retreat and withdrew his motion.

From time to time, I slipped up badly myself. At the end of a long speech defending Britain's economic performance against Soviet attack, I delivered a resounding and disastrous peroration. It began 'It is time to stop talking about the "recovery" of Britain. For us, the social and economic standards of prewar years are not things to be "recovered" but rather things to be repudiated,' and I went on to point out that we no longer had an unemployment problem, that the nation's health was better than ever before, and so on.

It all sounded fine to me, and indeed received some warm applause. But the fat was in the fire. I had forgotten that in Washington at that very moment the Senate was debating Britain's share of Marshall Plan aid, and all our friends were arguing that only a huge allocation of aid could save us from economic disaster. Britain's opponents joyfully seized on my speech and an emergency session of the Senate's Foreign Affairs Committee was summoned to discuss it. Sir Stafford Cripps, as Chancellor of the Exchequer, issued a statement ruthlessly repudiating me, and I became headline news on both sides of the Atlantic.

Brooding in my lonely hotel room, I calculated morbidly that my eloquent speech might well have cost the nation one and a half million dollars a word. However, some good men now came to my aid. A Foreign Office friend, Archie Mackenzie, dragged me from my hotel room and took me to dinner and an ice hockey match. Comforting telegrams arrived from Hector McNeil, James Callaghan and Ernest Bevin. Bevin's read:

Thank you for your very full statement. No harm was done except in the peroration. The thing to do in future is to avoid perorations. Do not worry too much: when you get into a tangle like this we old ones have to get you young ones out of trouble. Anyway, I understand the circs and don't let it daunt you. Good wishes.

The next day, high-ranking US officials persuaded the Senate committee that I had simply overreacted to 'needling' by the Russians and the crisis passed: but Arutiunian had the pleasure of informing the conference, in my presence, that my description of the British economy had been repudiated by my own government.

On the voyage home in the *Queen Mary*, at a party in the captain's cabin I was introduced to a charming Canadian woman. She opened the conversation: 'I am longing for the bad boy to arrive.' 'Bad boy?' I replied innocently. 'Yes, I am told he is coming – you know – the man who told the Americans we don't need any more Marshall dollars.' 'Oh,' I said, 'you mean *me*.'

On my return, Attlee stoutly defended me in the House, under heavy fire. Winston Churchill, the Leader of the Opposition, did not join in and came up to me afterwards at a reception. 'I think the newspapers have treated you very harshly,' he said, and moved away.

Throughout this time, I did not see Bevin often, but my admiration and affection for him grew steadily. At our first meeting following my appointment, after describing my duties, he said: 'Anything bad you do, I stand by you. Anything good you do, I take the credit. Get me a drink. Have one yourself.' It was this open, human attitude which endeared him to his subordinates. In addition, he was fearless in the face of criticism, and did not visit on us the anger and frustration he often felt against his numerous domestic and foreign enemies. Instead, we served as an audience for his colourful tirades – against Nye Bevan, Molotov, Herbert Morrison, Dick Crossman, the communists, the Zionists, the European federalists, the 'Keep Left' group.

In spite of this, Bevin's mind was also strongly creative, as is proved by his part in promoting the Marshall Plan, the Western European Union and NATO. He also kept cool at moments of crisis. I recall a meeting in his room at the time of the Berlin blockade. The Russians had cut off road and rail access to west Berlin and the Americans and British had fallen back on the desperate expedient of supplying the city with food and other essential resources by air. A few hours before our meeting, which was attended by the chiefs of staff, a British plane had been 'buzzed' by a Soviet fighter in one of the air corridors and had crashed with loss of life. The question Bevin had to decide was whether this was the beginning of a Soviet blockade of the air corridor, which would mean abandoning the airlift, followed almost certainly by war, or whether it was an accident. After much discussion, Bevin concluded, calmly and correctly, that in spite of appearances it must have been an accident.

Many years later, I suggested to Andrei Gromyko, then Soviet foreign minister, that this plane crash marked the most dangerous moment of the entire cold war. He agreed. (This, however, was before the Cuban crisis.)

I do not think that Bevin was ever wholeheartedly behind our propaganda offensive – less so, I judge, than Attlee and some other members of the Cabinet, and certainly less so than myself. But our relations were close, and he seemed to trust me. My diary for 15 December 1949 records:

EB has been unburdening himself a good deal. He has lost a lot of self-confidence. He said to me quite seriously last week 'Oh dear, what a failure I've been with everything. I do think I must give up.' I reassured him to the best of my ability. Palestine has been, and is, a terrible mess; and EB constantly feels he ought by now have got some kind of settlement with SU [the Soviet Union]. He's always been horribly optimistic about bringing the Soviet government to its senses, and blames himself for not bringing a settlement about. Too much wishful thinking about a settlement. No such thing is possible while SU is governed by Marxist-Leninists. Settlement utterly 'undialectical'. Only tactical truce possible, if that. [The] Soviet Union still thinks it has more to gain by trying to weaken and undermine the West than by trying to cooperate with us.

Apart from my efforts at the UN, I was naturally well placed to help disseminate IRD material within the British Labour movement. Here Denis Healey (now Lord Healey) played a key role. As secretary of the Labour Party's International Department, and himself a former communist, he was exceptionally well informed and sophisticated about anti-Soviet propaganda. I put him in touch with IRD officials and arranged for him to be sent all our material. I also arranged for his own admirable publications, critical of Stalinism, to be fed to suitable political and trade union contacts in foreign countries. Denis Healey always stoutly and rightly insisted that since Soviet communism treated social democracy as its main enemy, it was part of his duty, as

Labour's international secretary, to do his best to disseminate the truth about Stalinism.

In other directions, my efforts to help the IRD were less successful. One of our major allies should have been the British trade union movement. Besides being foreign secretary, Bevin was its most powerful leader, and the communists in the unions, though active and influential, were kept in check by stalwart right-wing bosses such as Arthur Deakin, Tom Williamson and Vincent Tewson.

The TUC might have seemed a natural outlet for IRD material. But it was cumbersome, ill-organized and short of finance. At this time, it was still affiliated to the communist-dominated World Federation of Trade Unions (WFTU). Plainly, it was not practicable to enlist the TUC officially in our anti-communist campaign.

However, an enterprising trade union official, Herbert Tracey, was already running an unofficial anti-communist organization within the unions called Freedom First, which had the backing of several influential union leaders and circulated a newsletter by the same name to 200 leading trade unionists. Tracey readily agreed that the IRD should supply material for the newsletter and purchase copies for overseas distribution. Later, we agreed that an international edition should be published, with mailing lists provided by labour attachés at our missions. Unfortunately, these plans miscarried when one of *Freedom First*'s major financial backers, Sydney Stanley, was exposed in the courts as a fraudster and fled to Israel to escape prosecution. For a time, *Freedom First* had to cease publication. Later, Tracey and I tried to reconstitute it. The international edition was never successful. Its tone was too strident; translation was expensive; and it was difficult to make it relevant to local trade union circumstances.

Other initiatives I took at this time were only partly successful. Quotable ministerial speeches were always particularly welcome. They received publicity without our assistance and could be readily used by the BBC. Early in 1948, I wrote round to a large number of sympathetic ministers and Labour MPs offering to send them IRD material. Almost all replied that they would welcome it, and I think that most of them would have read it and been heartened by it. But, in the event, few seemed to use it in their speeches. No doubt they found the same difficulty that we had found (and overcome) at the United Nations – the difficulty of initiating criticism of the Soviet Union without specific provocation.

I quite failed to persuade Bevin that the Labour Party – which was in favour of the idea – should summon an international conference of 15 European socialist parties to support the Marshall Plan against its communist enemies. Similarly, a proposal of mine to attach a social psychiatrist to the Foreign Office Russia Committee also came to nothing. This idea was not as eccentric as it sounded to many of my colleagues at the time: on the committee we were regularly trying to understand the unusual thought processes of the Soviet leaders – of Stalin especially – and to anticipate their decisions. To help us, we had an elaborate system of economic, political and diplomatic advisers but no one to assess the psychological factors. I was acquainted with a talented psychologist, Dr H. V. Dicks, who had done a valuable study for the War Office during the war on *Wehrmacht* morale and spoke fluent Russian; and, after much argument, I obtained agreement from my colleagues on the Russia Committee to approach him.

To my dismay, Dr Dicks informed me that he had received a very similar offer from the United States, where large-scale studies were being carried out. He felt that the task demanded a collective effort by a large number of people backed by adequate resources. He offered to ask the Americans if he could show us the results of his research, and I thanked him for this. It was clear we could not compete with the Americans. Dr Dicks was friendly and polite, but I felt somewhat chastened.

The archives remind me that in May 1949 I tried again to insert a positive element into our anti-communist publicity suggesting that we should publish a handbook similar to the successful *Points at Issue* but covering the constructive part of our foreign policy and the achievement of British social democracy. This, I knew, would be welcome to ministers, and the idea was vigorously supported by Patrick Gordon Walker. It was agreed in principle that the terms of reference of the Colonial Information Policy Committee, consisting of the parliamentary secretaries of the overseas departments, should be broadened to undertake this task.

However, it was also decided that the views of the principal embassies concerned should first be sought, and these proved to be uniformly unfavourable. The missions repeated their earlier objections to publicizing social democracy and also felt that they were already getting quite as much positive publicity material as they could handle. Consequently, for the second time, I bowed to the Foreign Office consensus and abandoned the idea that our anti-communist campaigning should include a positive element.

Over the years, the IRD's critics have been few but virulent. The first line of attack has been that our propaganda was distorted and misleading. In the *Guardian* of 19 August 1995, Mr Stephen Dorril wrote this about IRD: 'Black material – forgeries, lies and fabrications – was disseminated for use by MI6-funded radio stations and news agencies.'

On 21 August 1995, also in the *Guardian*, Mr Richard Gott wrote that the 'IRD's chief impact was to help poison the well-springs of British journalism and the independent study of international affairs for more than thirty years'.

A *Guardian* leader of 19 August 1995, written in Mr Gott's unmistakable style, took the same line. Headed 'Disinformation and FO Gold', it attacked the IRD's 'subtle tainting of some scholarship and journalism'.

However, common to all the IRD's critics, was their remarkable failure to quote a single example of the lies and fabrications they alleged. In one form or another, the IRD must have published millions of words, and all are now available to its critics; yet not a single inaccuracy – let alone a lie or fabrication – has been brought to light. This is a remarkable tribute to the IRD's practice of researching a subject thoroughly and sticking to the truth.

After all, what need was there to exaggerate or distort the evils of Stalinism? It would have been neither necessary nor sensible. Telling the truth was enough.

The critics had a second line of attack: the IRD's propaganda campaign was covert – it was financed by the government but never openly attributed to it. This is true, and in normal circumstances would be objectionable. But the circumstances of the cold war were not normal. They meant that communism (unlike democratic creeds such as conservatism or democratic socialism) became a legitimate target for publicly financed government propaganda. During the cold war, there were MPs in Westminster – some of them open or secret members of the Communist Party – who could and would have attacked our campaign if ministers had been made answerable for it in Parliament. The Labour government took the robust and correct view that where the defence of democracy was concerned, minor and temporary deviations from normal parliamentary practice were legitimate and necessary. In the same way, when the communists were opposing the war against Hitler and doing their best to impede war production, the government deviated from the democratic norm and banned the *Daily Worker*.

The critics' final objection to the IRD is that its methods resembled those of the Soviet Union. The *Guardian*, 19 August 1995, declared 'IRD's defence is that the Soviets were doing it too. Is that really adequate, and was not "our side" supposed to have higher standards?' Stephen Dorril (*Guardian*, 18 August 1995) asserts that 'the moral high ground was lost as soon as the tactics used became no different from those of the Soviet propagandists.'

Thus, the critics equate the IRD's methods with those of the Soviet Union, as though the IRD twisted the truth and underpinned its propaganda by censoring newspapers and books, jamming broadcasts and suppressing dissident opinions of every kind. The IRD did none of these things, and the Soviet government did all of them; and the fact that the *Guardian* fails to make this distinction casts doubt on its liberal pretensions. The doubts are strengthened by the *Guardian*'s placing of 'our side' in inverted commas: which tallies with the newspaper's ambivalent stand throughout much of the cold war, with the surreptitious presence of a KGB contact – Richard Gott – on its editorial board, and with its commissioning of far left columnists to attack the IRD.

How much, in the end, did the IRD achieve? It is difficult to assess this. How many million listeners in how many countries heard BBC broadcasts containing IRD material? How many millions of foreigners read articles commissioned by the IRD in their own language in their own newspapers? How many scores of thousands read our briefing papers? Many of these papers would undoubtedly be laid aside unread, or read only by the information officer to whom they had been sent. Many would have been read but ignored. But we know – to take one example – that our very first briefing paper, 'The real conditions in the

Propaganda and the Workers' Paradise

Soviet Union', was translated by the Dutch Labour Party and distributed to its 30,000 members. This was certainly not a unique reaction. Since there were hundreds of papers in this series, and each was published in hundreds of copies, the briefs must have reached an army of readers directly or indirectly and must have had a major impact.

The papers also reached some remote places. In August 1995, after *The Times* had published a letter from me about the IRD, an old friend of mine, Tony Harrison, wrote:

When I was deputy High Commissioner in Peshawar in 1956–9 I used to receive small batches of IRD prints from our High Commissioner in Karachi.

I used to visit the Pakistani Director General of Police in Peshawar who was concerned with intelligence on the frontier. He was of course highly suspicious of Soviet activities and intentions in Afghanistan and on the frontier. I would show, or give him copies of, selected IRD prints and he quite often commented 'this will be very useful to me.'

But the usefulness of IRD's information was, I think, only part of its value. This Pakistani policeman might or might not have passed on – to like-minded politicians or to a local newspaper – IRD's information about the Soviet invasion of Hungary or some such subject. But he would certainly have been heartened by this evidence that in his efforts to defeat the campaign against communism he had some committed well-informed people on his side, wanting to help him.[10]

The same was true, I think, of the impact of IRD material nearer home. At Westminster, a Labour MP or trade union leader might or might not pass on the information in an IRD paper, but he would be encouraged by the knowledge that he had well-informed allies, and would be readier to stand up to communist pressure in his constituency party or trade union branch.

Much of the IRD's success depended on the keenness and ability of the IRD representative on the spot and the quality of his or her local contacts. We had no control – and little information – beyond that point. Most of his contacts would be committed anti-communists, and he would have little difficulty there in providing them with the information they needed and wanted. Sometimes, they were over-enthusiastic. Sir Hugh Greene recalled that when he was in Malaya in the early 1950s, sometimes as many as three anti-communist articles would appear in one issue of the *Malay Mail*. 'It seemed that space was being filled with free material. It was rather overdone and might be counterproductive in that it would have raised some eyebrows.' But Greene never felt that there was anything at all 'dirty' about IRD, but rather 'a certain clumsiness in the use of material because, presumably, they would not be able to control this'.[11]

After I left the IRD in 1950, it continued to expand rapidly. In 1949, its staff totalled 53; by the early 1960s it numbered about 200 and by the end of the 1960s about 300, when it was cut back by more than half by Norman Reddaway as deputy director. It also moved from Riverwalk House in Millbank to the main Foreign Office building.

By then, propaganda against communism had become only one of its tasks. More controversially, it played a key role, under Reddaway's guidance, in a publicity campaign that resulted in the removal of Achmed Sukarno as president of Indonesia, in 1965/6, and in propagating the reasons for voting yes in the Common Market referendum in 1972.

At a critical moment, an important meeting was held between Cabinet Secretary Norman Brook, Pat Dean representing the Foreign Office, the director of MI5, Mr (later Sir) Roger Hollis, and Norman Reddaway representing the IRD. At the end of it, Brook instructed Hollis to make available to the Foreign Office, with security collateral, intelligence about communist malpractices in the unions that could be used by the IRD. This led, among other things, to the ousting of Foulkes and Haxell from the leadership of the electrical trades union.

The IRD was born under a Labour government: it was also wound up under a Labour government. On 13 April 1977, Dr David Owen, as foreign secretary, closed it down.

In the late 1940s and the 1950s, the IRD was of critical importance. There were times when we thought that the communists might win power even in Paris and Rome. This was not due to economic or military pressure, but to aggressive ideological warfare. If this had gone a little further, and if the Marshall Plan had not succeeded, much of western Europe might have gone the way of eastern Europe.

The IRD can probably claim a modest share of the credit for

stemming and turning back the Soviet ideological offensive. It did help to destroy Stalinist illusions. It gave encouragement to people who wished to tell the truth about the Soviet Union and it helped to blunt the impact of Stalinist political warfare. In the United Nations, in the Third World, in Malaysia, and in many other countries, it heartened people who were doing their best to resist the propaganda of Stalin. It also helped people at home who were tangling with fellow-travellers and the like; and it played a major part in getting rid of communist influence in key trade unions. I was told many times how the material was used and greatly appreciated. The IRD was able to let informed people know the facts and I think that this helped to maintain democracy and that, after all, was our primary aim.

Chapter 3
The Cultural Cold War

After the 1950 general election, having lost my seat and consequently my Foreign Office job, and having decided to hold out for a by-election, I was in a position to satisfy an unusual ambition. During the long sessions at the Economic and Social Council of the United Nations, devoted to drafting the UN Declaration of Human Rights, I had become fascinated by the contrast between the eloquent speeches of the Soviet delegates, extolling freedom in communist countries, and the strict regimentation of their personal lives by the KGB. So I decided to try to write a TV play dramatizing this contrast. I had particularly in mind a successful Soviet amendment to Article 12 of the draft declaration, which added 'privacy of correspondence' to the other protected human rights.

The plot of the play would be as follows: gathering up his scattered papers at the end of a session of the Council, the British delegate unknowingly sweeps up a letter written by his neighbour, the Soviet delegate, to his wife, in which he complains about the oppressive discipline imposed on Soviet delegates by the KGB. The British delegate is urged by his advisers to use the letter for propaganda purposes, but refuses. The terrified Soviet delegate visits him secretly, begs for the letter back and gets it; but he is suspected by the KGB of being about to defect and is murdered. The play ends as the Council unanimously votes for the Soviet amendment to add 'privacy of correspondence' to the Declaration of Human Rights.

If I read the play today, I blush for shame at the clumsiness of the dialogue. For example, after handing back the letter, the British delegate (played by Andrew Cruickshank) admonishes the wretched Russian:

If there is anything certain in the world it is that you and your friends, with your trivial, trite, little relativist philosophy, you'll come to grief in due course, like all your predecessors. Respect for truth, a sense of justice, tolerance, mercy – you've liquidated them all. And all this has happened so often before. In the mind of history, the corruption of your empire will be a commonplace, its downfall a matter of routine.

Emphatically, this is not the way one man normally talks to another in private conversation. But poor Andrew Cruickshank made the best of it and, in 1951, it sounded rather splendid; it has certainly proved prescient.

The *Daily Worker* devoted a leading article to the play: 'In the unctuous tones of the unco guid, Mr Mayhew claims that his play illustrates the superiority of those animated by Christian principle on the one hand over those who deny God on the other. In reality the play is the most vicious and disgusting anti-Soviet propaganda yet put across by the BBC.'

However, other reviewers liked it, and so, according to audience research, did the viewers. It was rebroadcast in the United States by CBS, who shamelessly changed the British delegate into an American delegate without changing his lines in any way.

After this modest success, I began to fancy myself as a Kremlinologist and, when Stalin died in 1953, I rashly volunteered to write a radio play for the BBC dramatizing the first meeting of the members of the Politburo after the dictator's death.

Much taken by this idea, the BBC scheduled the play for the Overseas Service, to be followed by a repeat on the Home Service.

After consulting other students of Soviet affairs, I wrote the play quickly and confidently, basing it on the assumption that there was a close understanding between Prime Minister Georgiy Malenkov and his Minister for Internal Security, Lavrenti Beria.

The broadcast went well and I received a warm letter of congratulations from Gordon Mosley, the director of overseas services. Then, a few days later, I received my comeuppance: with Malenkov's ready agreement, Beria was murdered.

The scheduled Home Service broadcast was hastily scrapped; and on my next visit to the Soviet embassy, an official murmured in my ear, 'Been writing any more plays recently, Mr Mayhew?'

However, this well-deserved setback in no way lessened my interest in Soviet affairs. In the following year, I revisited the Soviet Union as a member of a high-level official parliamentary delegation.

We travelled with complete freedom wherever we chose to go, and met and questioned scores of Soviet citizens, including the Soviet leaders.

At the end of it all, I was far from reassured. I was particularly distrustful of the proclaimed new objectives of Soviet foreign policy. These were, it is true, a major improvement on the classical statements of Stalin and Lenin. In his book *Problems of Leninism* (1945 edition), Stalin had stated:

The revolution which has been victorious in one country must regard itself not as a self-sufficient entity but as an aid, a means of hastening the victory of the proletariat in all countries. For the victory of the revolution in one country, in the present case Russia, is ... the beginning of, and the groundwork for, the world revolution.

Foolish as this was, it was less so than Lenin's famous statement, familiar to every Soviet schoolchild:

The victorious proletariat of the Soviet Union, having expropriated the capitalists and organized its own socialist production, would stand up against the rest of the world, the capitalist world, attracting to its cause the oppressed classes of other countries, raising revolts in those countries against the capitalists, and in the event of necessity coming out, even with armed force, against the exploiting classes and their states.

To the British parliamentary delegation, seated decorously round the long table in Malenkov's office in the Kremlin, it seemed a far cry from these reckless statements to Malenkov's and Molotov's courteous dissertations on 'peace', 'coexistence' and 'friendship'. And, indeed, it was plain that the ideas of Lenin and Stalin had been considerably modified – not least by the omission of any reference to armed force –

and made considerably more acceptable to Western ears. But when probed, the new concepts still suffered from the disastrous basic errors of Marxism: they still assumed that the world was inevitably divided between two camps – the socialist camp and the capitalist camp; that confrontation between them was inevitable, and that the socialist camp would inevitably prevail. In the minds of the Soviet leadership, 'peace', 'friendship' and 'coexistence' had a specific purpose with which the West was still unfamiliar: they were the concepts with which the Soviet Union, in Lenin's words, would 'attract to its cause the oppressed classes of other countries'. In the minds of the Soviet leaders, they were the best way, in the nuclear age, of forwarding the victory of world socialism.

To me, they seemed divisive and disruptive, certain to undermine rather than promote *détente* between East and West.

During our tour of the Soviet Union, I became particularly interested in the Soviet concept of 'friendship'. Here, there seemed to be practical remedies. I began to think I might even contribute to them myself.

At the direct personal level, the Russians meant by 'friendship' exactly what everyone else meant. Everywhere the delegation went, we had a warm, touchingly sincere welcome from the Soviet people, which we heartily reciprocated. Broad smiles and delighted clapping followed us from farm to farm and factory to factory. Sometimes I asked one of our embassy interpreters to eavesdrop on the comments of bystanders, and these too were respectful of us, sometimes in a revealing way. 'How clean they are – you can tell they are not ours.' 'How democratic of them, coming to Gorki market on foot.'

When we asked people how they felt about Britain, they all gave the same, obviously sincere, answers. Their feelings towards the British people, they declared, were of the warmest friendship. In particular, they admired our struggle for peace, led by their courageous peace fighters – and here they would name British communists and fellow travellers, such as Dr Hewlett Johnson (Dean of Canterbury), Konni Zilliacus, MP, D. N. Pritt, MP, and Pat Sloan, secretary of the British–Soviet Friendship Society (BSFS). They explained that they wished the British people well in their struggle for friendship with the Soviet Union against the forces of American and British capitalism.

It became apparent that the British people for whom the Russians expressed friendship were – though they did not know it – very largely a figment of their imagination. They consisted almost entirely of class-conscious proletarians who admired the Dean of Canterbury and supported the Soviet Union's peace policy, who fought heroically against the forces of British and American capitalism and, if only voting were free and the press were fair, would return a majority of communist MPs to Parliament.

I began to see that the normalization of British–Soviet relations involved outright opposition to the Soviet concept of 'friendship' and to the pro-Soviet British citizens who practised it.

These British citizens themselves took a Marxist view of Britain. They read (and often wrote for) the *Daily Worker*, and talked that language to the Russians they met. From their ranks came the authors who wrote the only newspaper articles and books about Britain that the Russians were allowed to read. They supplied a wholly disproportionate share of tourists and 'delegates' to communist countries. The damage they did – sometimes no doubt unintentionally – in misleading Russians about Britain was very serious.

The organizations that did most of the damage were the BSFS and the Society for Cultural Relations (SCR). Both were presided over by winners of the Stalin peace prize, and run by a hard core of British Communist Party members. Another important organization in this field was the British Youth Festival Committee. No visitor to the Soviet Union who probed beneath the surface could fail to see signs of the damage that these organizations did – in confirming Soviet misconceptions of Britain and of the outside world.

A teacher in a Moscow school, hoping to reassure me, explained that they sometimes heard the British point of view expressed by British people on Moscow radio. 'Do you remember the names of any of these broadcasters?' I asked. He replied with the name of a well-known British communist, Mr Ivor Montagu.

Outside my hotel in Moscow, I was buttonholed by two English-speaking students. We went and had a fruit juice in a nearby restaurant. They said they had helped with the Moscow Youth Festival, and had had many frank political talks with British 'delegates'. Later, I asked them to guess the number of members of the British Communist

ABOVE. Christopher Mayhew at a Fabian Summer school, 1938.

RIGHT. Christopher Mayhew was Under Secretary to the British Foreign Minister, Ernest Bevin, 1946-50.

3. & 4. LEFT & BELOW
Newly appointed at the
Foreign Office,
Christopher Mayhew at
work, 1945-6

6. RIGHT & BELOW
home in Wilton Street,
7-8.

7. ABOVE. Christopher and Cicely Mayhew with (far right) Amazap Arutiunian, Soviet representative at the UN.

8. LEFT. As part of a parliamentary delegation Christopher Mayhew revisited the Soviet Union in 1954.

9 & 10. ABOVE & RIGHT.
Meeting Soviet factory
workers, 1954.

11. LEFT. Bangkok, 1955: 'countering Soviet effort to win Third World countries by propaganda'

12. BELOW. Signing the 1960 US-UK co-operation agreement against Soviet front organisations

3. ABOVE. Visiting the headquarters, Allied Forces Central Europe, Fontainebleau, France, September 1961.

4. RIGHT. As Minister of Defence for the Royal Navy, Christopher Mayhew visited NATO's headquarters of the Supreme Allied Commander Atlantic, January 1965.

15. LEFT. Christopher Mayhew was raised to th peerage in 1981.

16. BELOW. Christopher Mayhew's eighth visit to the Soviet Union, with David Steel and Russell Johnston, took place in 1984.

Party. After some hesitation, one of them said 'one million'; whereupon the other quickly interposed, 'no, far more'. The actual figure at the time was about 35,000.

I found the Soviet Ministry of Culture apparently quite happy that cultural relations between our countries should be conducted by the communist-led friendship societies. I pointed out to a high official that the individuals running these societies in Britain were so unrepresentative and unpopular that no member of the parliamentary delegation would associate with them in any way; and that British–Soviet friendship should surely be put on a firmer basis. The official stoutly defended the societies and those who were running them: while it was good to have friendship with non-communists, it was still more important to encourage the courageous people who were proven supporters of the Soviet Union.

These errors of judgement were natural to Marxists. Believers in historical determinism, they tended to confuse what they were sure was coming into being with what actually existed. I found my insistence that the British working class was not pro-Soviet and class-conscious was put down to my undialectical approach, my failure to grasp the underlying dynamic of British capitalist society.

Marxist misconceptions of this kind naturally encouraged the belief that the Soviet Union had more to gain by fostering the struggle of the British working class against capitalism than by cooperating with Britain's capitalist governments. On my return home from the Soviet Union I decided to try to do something to dispel this disastrous illusion.

It was clear, however, that personal encounters on level terms between representative (non-Marxist) British people and representative (Marxist) Russians did help towards mutual understanding. Indeed, I felt that the visit of our parliamentary delegation had confirmed this. For example, led by Dick Law (later Lord Colcraine), a former Conservative Cabinet minister, we had particularly stressed the damage done to East–West relations by the Soviet Union's support for foreign communist parties through the Cominform. It was difficult to press this strongly at our formal meetings with the Soviet leaders, but at our farewell reception, Dick Law and I questioned Molotov and Gromyko about it frankly and in some detail. I made a note of the conversation.

A War of Words

GROMYKO: We do not support foreign communist parties.
CM: The parties themselves plainly say that they look to Russia for leadership.
GROMYKO: We just give them moral support, that is all. You think all communist parties are agents of the Soviet Union, but they arise out of objective conditions.
CM: On the average, they are 70 per cent natural growths, 30 per cent Soviet creations, and the 30 per cent is a great cause of international friction.
GROMYKO: I think you have your mathematical proportions wrong.
MOLOTOV: (*coming up*) I see that Gromyko is one against two.
LAW: He is well able to look after himself.
MOLOTOV: So are you two, I believe.
GROMYKO: As usual, the strongest attacks have come from the left.
MOLOTOV: Have you seen everything you wanted?
CM: Everything except one thing.
MOLOTOV: What is that?
CM: A communist party.
MOLOTOV: (*laughing*) We are all communists.
CM: We have visited the headquarters of trade unions, city councils – but never the headquarters of a communist party. We find the communist parties very shy.
MOLOTOV: (*laughing*) We are all communists – there is no point in meeting the Communist Party.
LAW: We have been discussing the question of your support for foreign communist parties.
MOLOTOV: What do you mean?
CM: Your leadership of these parties through the Cominform, the circulation of unfriendly literature printed in Russia.
MOLOTOV: What literature?
CM: *New Times*, for example.
MOLOTOV: (*laughing*) But that is bought openly by people. It is perfectly legitimate.
CM: The award of a Lenin peace prize to the Dean of Canterbury.
MOLOTOV: The Dean is a fighter for peace.

CM:	Should we not define our terms? Your fighters for peace supported North Korea's invasion of South Korea. They are a very warlike crew. Might I offer a definition of peace?

(*Molotov nodded*)

CM:	Peace is any state of affairs, including war, which forwards Mr Molotov's foreign policy.
MOLOTOV:	(*laughing*) The Soviet Union is so strong that no attacks on her can succeed. Equally, she has no cause to attack others. We must learn to talk a common language and conduct our affairs in a friendly and sensible manner.
LAW:	But Britain and the United States are separated by a common language.
MOLOTOV:	The United States is conducting subversive operations in eastern Europe.
CM:	Do the Americans have a right to do this, just as you support communist activities?
MOLOTOV:	We are not doing in the Western world what the Americans are attempting in eastern Europe. The Cominform is simply an information bureau, not the same as the old Comintern. It exists to carry out certain ties between communist parties in Europe. There are similar ties between socialist parties. We consider this to be quite natural. The Cominform and its ties are designed to secure peace in Europe. It is a matter for the parties which form it. The Soviet government is not part of the Cominform.

(*Molotov and Law then moved away, but Gromyko continued*)

GROMYKO:	But you can see for yourself how Marxism has proved itself in history.
CM:	Isn't it a question of definitions? For example, the hypothesis that Russia is a democratic workers' state, opposed by world capitalism. You maintain this only by defining those who support Russia as democrats and workers, and those who oppose it as capitalists. Thus Tito was a worker one day and a capitalist the next.

GROMYKO: But see how Marxism has spread and is spreading throughout the world. And what other philosophy are you putting against it? Who are the philosophers in Britain?

I should have replied that there were many different schools of philosophy in Britain, but instead mentioned Russell and Ayer, and said they seemed to be concerned with the meaning of words. What philosophical work had been done in Russia since Lenin?

GROMYKO: Lenin was right – we apply his teachings. What is your philosophy? Is this glass I am holding 'real' or not?

CM: My grandparents felt sure it was 'real'. Now, modern science has led us to have doubts. Our minds and senses have more to do with the creation of what we call the natural world than we thought.

GROMYKO: That is interesting – the way in which the findings of modern science can lead to two totally different interpretations.

At that time, frank conversations of this kind were unprecedented. Whether they made any impression on the Soviet leaders is hard to judge; but in fact, for whatever reason, they abolished the Cominform shortly after our visit. For the British, the talks made clearer than before which practices the Soviet leaders regarded as legitimate, or illegitimate, in their promotion of world communism. At the time, this was valuable information.

In addition, our delegation found that contacts that were entirely non-political could generate real goodwill and mutual respect. One of our members was Gerald Wellesley, seventh Duke of Wellington, an elderly, upright and modest person with no interest in politics at all. However, as a direct descendant of the revered conqueror of Napoleon I, he commanded immense interest and respect in Russian eyes. He had served in the British embassy in St Petersburg during the First World War and spoke perfect Russian. On one occasion, as we gathered on the terrace of the Tsar's Winter Palace, he remarked quietly to a thunderstruck Russian guide that the last time he had stood on that terrace, the Tsar himself had served him coffee.

Towards the end of our visit, the Duke asked me to accompany him to a museum – formerly a country house – outside Moscow. He explained that after the battle of Waterloo, the first duke had taken possession of two magnificent Sèvres dinner services, commissioned by Napoleon to commemorate his invasion of Egypt, and had presented one set to the Tsar, keeping the other for himself. The seventh Duke now wished to compare the Tsar's set with his own. We were greeted by the museum's staff with understandable amazement and joy, and hastened to begin the long task of expert comparison. At one point I remember the Duke, consulting his huge volume of photographs, remarked that the museum's set lacked one of his sauce boats. The museum staff seemed undismayed by this, and the visit itself enchanted both sides.

During the delegation's tour, there were similar meetings of this kind, though none so colourful. It was obvious that non-political cultural contacts could make a substantial contribution to genuine friendship between the two peoples.

By a stroke of good fortune I was at this time a member of the executive committee of the British Council, and I thought the best way forward would be to form a specialist Soviet relations committee of the British Council. Its task would be to promote contacts of all kinds with the Soviet Union, on a representative basis, squeezing out the Marxist-led friendship societies.

Plainly, we would need Foreign Office support. This would ensure our financing, and make available the contacts of the Foreign Office and of our embassy in Moscow. We must have enough authority to fulfil our task while remaining independent and non-governmental. I put this idea to Robin Turton, then parliamentary under-secretary at the Foreign Office, who evidently liked it.

I also wrote to newspaper editors and other influential people, including Sir Ian Jacob, director-general of the BBC. In his reply, having thanked me for a copy of a relevant newspaper article I had written, he continued: 'I very strongly agree with your general thesis. It is an impossible situation that we should deal with these visitors through the medium of "front" organizations. It is a question to which we have been giving a good deal of thought, because it also affects traffic in the opposite direction.'[1]

A War of Words

I was greatly encouraged by Jacob's reaction, and asked him to repeat his view to the Foreign Office. Other key people also responded enthusiastically, including Clem Attlee.

On 10 May 1955, the project was launched in an official Foreign Office statement. A new committee of the British Council was to be set up, under my chairmanship, with Mr C. E. Mott-Radclyffe MP, chairman of the Conservative Parliamentary Foreign Affairs Committee, as vice-chairman. Other members of the committee included Sir Paul Sinker, director-general of the British Council; a moderate trade union leader, Sir Vincent Tewson; and the head of the Foreign Office Northern Department, Harry Hohler.

So far so good. Soon I was able to issue an invitation to the Soviet minister of culture, Mr Mikhailov, on behalf of a dazzling array of leading cultural and educational establishments, to visit Britain to agree a policy and programme for British–Soviet cultural exchanges.

Mr Mikhailov accepted my invitation. This was something of a breakthrough. It also marked the beginning of a bizarre 'cultural cold war'. Both sides genuinely wanted to increase cultural contacts, but disagreed sharply about their nature and purpose. The Russians valued organized contacts as a means of promoting Soviet communism and as a cover-up for their ruthless suppression of genuinely free communications. In the Soviet Union, foreign newspapers, unless communist, were banned. Foreign broadcasts were jammed. Foreign books were vetted. Foreign travel, where permitted at all, was tightly controlled. When Mr Mikhailov or some other Soviet cultural bureaucrat raised his glass to 'the removal of barriers between our two peoples', no one supposed for a moment that he meant it seriously.

But there was humbug on the British side too. We spoke warmly about Count Leo Nikolayevich Tolstoy and Robert Burns, David Oistrakh and Benjamin Britten, but our aims were political: we wanted to break down the isolation of the Soviet people from the West and to disrupt their ties with British communists and fellow-travellers.

Neither side had any illusions about the other. I rightly regarded Mr Mikhailov, Mr Surkov (secretary of the Soviet Writers' Union) and Mr Zhukov (chairman of the State Committee for Cultural Relations with Foreign Countries) as friends of the British 'left' and enemies of cultural freedom. They saw me, rightly, as a hardened cold warrior. They did business with the Soviet Relations Committee (SRC) only because they had to, because otherwise their cultural and educational delegations were likely to be cold-shouldered by their British equivalents and ignored by the media. At one time they entreated the Foreign Office to have me removed as chairman of the SRC. Apparently, the complaint about me was that I did not have a 'warm heart'. But this request was firmly resisted by the Foreign Office.

Mr Mikhailov's arrival at Heathrow on 1 February 1956 was an apt presage of things to come. Predictably, he made a speech at the airport calling for the removal of barriers to friendship and understanding between Britain and the Soviet Union. Anticipating this, I had arranged for the BBC external services to record the speech and broadcast it to the Soviet Union, where, of course, it was jammed. So, the next day, at our first formal meeting, I asked Mr Mikhailov whether he approved of his eloquent appeal for free contacts being jammed by his government. He replied with a smile that this was a matter for another department. He took my provocation in good part, and may even have taken some action afterwards: jamming of the BBC was temporarily suspended when Nikita Khrushchev and Marshal Nikolay Bulganin visited Britain the following year.

During our first formal meeting, I pointed out that the SRC was the only organization capable of handling exchanges on the basis of goodwill on both sides. Also, that while the SRC could do much good work, it was only a second best to the establishment of free normal cultural relations and contacts with the Soviet Union on the model of our contacts with, for example, Canada, France and India, where free contacts could be made between person to person. Such was our aim with the Soviet Union and I asked Mikhailov if this was also his objective. Mr Mikhailov responded that the Soviet aim was the all-round strengthening and development of cultural ties and that, in the future, they aimed to develop personal contacts, including tourism as well as exchanges between students and professors, and assured us that, given goodwill on both sides, much could be done. He added that arrangements for the recent visit of the Moiseyev ensemble had not been satisfactory.

A War of Words

This provided me with a useful opening: I mentioned that the Moiseyev dancers had come under the auspices of the British–Soviet Friendship Society (BSFS), a society of an ideological nature controlled by British members of the Communist Party and sympathizers. Had the SRC been asked to organize the visit, arrangements would have been on a more efficient basis, since British theatre managers were ready to cooperate with the committee but reluctant to work with the BSFS. I went on to point out that this applied not only to the theatrical world but to broadcasting, political parties, universities and professional organizations of all kinds.

Mr Mikhailov assured us that the Soviet aim was the strengthening of cultural ties with all countries, including Great Britain, and that the Ministry of Culture had no monopoly. He mentioned the contacts that had been made with trade unions, professional organizations, the British Council's committee and the BSFS and how the Soviet Union felt the widest possible base was in the interest of the further development of contacts.

It was at this stage, I believe, that I came nearest to being popular with the Soviet cultural bureaucracy. There was a highly successful song and dance display by the Soviet army at the Empress Hall in London at which the ambassador, Mr Jacob Malik, came very near to congratulating me. He did in fact go so far as to say: 'It gives us great satisfaction to mark their first performance here as an important landmark in the great and noble work of developing British–Soviet cultural relations and cooperation.' Avoiding politics, I got a big cheer for saying: 'All of us, I am sure, would think it a happy day if all military formations everywhere were permanently engaged in singing and dancing.' Nevertheless, Mr Malik and I, though remaining on quite friendly personal terms, had no illusions at all about the underlying political conflict between us.

I was adamant about the need for reciprocity in British–Soviet exchanges. Invited by telegram to contribute an article on the Bulganin–Khrushchev visit for the English-language periodical *News*, I replied 'Appreciate offer. Am always glad contribute Soviet papers, but unwilling contribute Soviet papers in English circulating Britain until reciprocal freedom granted British papers in Russian circulating Soviet Union.'

The Cultural Cold War

I was equally 'hardline' with the British friendship societies, which would write to me in conciliatory style suggesting mutual cooperation. I was perfectly clear that if we were to maintain the trust of the representative British organizations with whom we dealt, as well as the trust of the government and opposition in Parliament, it was essential to keep a sizeable distance between us. I have no doubt that the organizers of the 'friendship' societies – if not their members – fully understood this position. There were setbacks of course. For example, when the Moiseyev folk dancers came over I took the usual course of warning the BBC and other organizations and individuals about their auspices and they all agreed to cold-shoulder them. But then, to my dismay, I discovered that they were booked to appear before royalty. So, after a cool brush-off from the palace ('Her Majesty does not intervene in political questions'), I had to go into reverse, losing credibility as a result.

There were other uncomfortable moments. I remember the chairman of the SCR, Mr John Platts-Mills, at a reception in the Soviet embassy, crossing the floor to greet me. I declined his handshake and turned aside. This was difficult to do. He was an amiable fellow, a former Labour MP, and we were on Christian name terms. But I was determined that the Soviet embassy officials should understand how the land lay.

It was nevertheless proving easier to persuade the Russians to develop new contacts than to give up their old ties with the 'friendship' societies, and eventually I asked John Selwyn Lloyd, then foreign secretary, to raise this question with the two Soviet leaders, Bulganin and Khrushchev, on their visit to Britain in April 1956. I urged him to insert the following formula into the official communiqué: 'The two governments accept the need for organizing these exchanges in a manner acceptable to them both.'

At the Speaker's lunch for Bulganin and Khrushchev, Mikhailov hurried up to me and explained anxiously that every word of the communiqué had been agreed except one point. The point was, of course, my formula. He said he had discussed this with Bulganin and Khrushchev, and both had urged that it should be dropped from the communiqué. I said, on the contrary, this was the most important part of the communiqué and was an essential condition for future cooperation on cultural relations.

When lunch was over, Prime Minister Anthony Eden himself came up to me and said that he had spent a good deal of the morning with Bulganin and Khrushchev on my formula. He thought it was very toughly worded. I said it was not tough at all, but plain common sense. If the Russians would not accept it, it showed it was all the more important to insist on it. He said I must speak to Bulganin myself about it and led me over to the marshal. I put the case to Bulganin and after reflection he said, in the Prime Minister's hearing, 'I accept'.

I heard no more until a special performance was held at Covent Garden for Bulganin and Khrushchev. This had been laid on by the Soviet Relations Committee and I found myself their host. Eden and Selwyn Lloyd were the other guests, with the two ambassadors. As I entered the foyer, the Prime Minister came up and began talking earnestly about my formula, saying that he and Bulganin and Khrushchev had again spent considerable time on it that afternoon. He said that Bulganin had given some important assurances. I said, 'You mean you've dropped the formula.' He said rather shamefacedly that he had, but that the assurances were important. I said I didn't trust Bulganin and Khrushchev an inch. He warmly agreed with this but said, 'There was really nothing else we could do.' Then, seeing that I was pretty adamant, he said, 'If they do let us down again, then we shall be in a good position to start denying visas when they use these communist societies.' When I remained unmoved, he said, 'Well you must talk to them yourself over dinner.'

I waited until the second interval, when we were at supper behind the royal box, and then tackled Bulganin. I was feeling like Walter Mitty in one of his daydreams, with these powerful figures notably anxious about what was, after all, little more than my own personal opinion. I began by referring to the constructive work we had done in the cultural field in the past 12 months. However, it was quite inadmissible that the Soviet authorities should use communist-controlled organizations to forward cultural relations between our countries. For this reason, a formula had been suggested which Marshal Bulganin would probably know as Clause 7. I understood that this formula had been conceded by the government in return for certain assurances from Marshal Bulganin. Both the opposition and my committee felt even more strongly in favour of the principle behind the formula than the government itself. I felt sure that if the opposition raised this question in Parliament, they would get unusually wide parliamentary support. (This was for Eden and Selwyn Lloyd, who were listening keenly.) I would like to be able to assure the opposition and the committee about the nature of Marshal Bulganin's assurances.

Bulganin said he would very readily explain it to me exactly. He said that he recognized that they had not a sufficient understanding of this problem before. He undertook that when he returned to Moscow he would look into the question with a view to making possible changes.

I said, 'To take a specific example, though, I believe you have been discussing the question of the Moscow Circus (due to visit Britain shortly under the auspices of the British–Soviet Friendship Society) this afternoon. This would surely be a good point of departure.' Bulganin made the hopeful reply, 'When is the circus due?' I told him 12 May, and he nodded. I then said, 'Let us enlist the animals in the cause of British–Soviet friendship,' at which he laughed. After a pause he then said to me, with flattering earnestness, 'Do you accept my assurances?'

I had worked it out that his assurances were not worth very much. Moreover, our parliamentary position, if we attacked the government for its utter feebleness, would be extraordinarily strong. On the other hand, Eden's assurance about visas was important, and we were in any case gaining the ascendancy in this cultural cold war. Finally, if I resigned, the constructive work we had been achieving would be largely wasted. So I replied, 'I am sure that when Marshal Bulganin returns to Moscow he will lay the foundation for future cooperation in this cultural field.' The evident relief of Khrushchev, Bulganin, Selwyn Lloyd and Eden at this statement by a backbench MP was gratifying in the extreme.

A few days after this, the Moscow Circus abruptly tore up its contract with the BSFS and, although the Soviet government never completely severed its ties with the 'friendship' organizations, its support for them thereafter fell away.

Khrushchev made a most favourable impression on me. He reminded me of Ernest Bevin – burly, coarse-featured, boisterous, humorous, outgoing, shrewd. At one moment during supper, he put down his knife and fork and said: 'I will now tell an anti-Soviet story.' After waiting until he saw that we were all listening – including the Prime Minister and the Foreign Secretary – he went on.

There were once two friends who shared a flat in Moscow. One was a professor of literature and the other a secret police chief. One evening the professor came home and said to his friend, 'My friend, this has been the worst day of my life: I asked one of my pupils, "Who wrote War and Peace*?" and he replied, "Honestly, professor, I didn't." Away went the police chief and came back a fortnight later. 'It's all right,' he said to his friend, 'I found that student. He has confessed. He* did *write* War and Peace.*'*

Since Khrushchev himself had certainly used, or connived at, the most brutal methods of repression during his career in the Soviet Communist Party, this story had grim echoes for his British listeners. But Khrushchev had recently made his famous anti-Stalin speech at the twentieth party conference, which told in his favour, and the fact that he wished to convey his opposition to Stalinist methods to the British Prime Minister and Foreign Secretary seemed to me, in the climate of those days, a healthy step forward.

I remember too that, as a leaving gift, Khrushchev presented me with, among other things, five albums of Soviet gramophone records. I knew nothing about Soviet records, and was saddened, but not surprised, when the sound quality of the first one I tried turned out to be extremely poor. I assumed that this was another example of the notoriously low standard of Soviet consumer goods. A few days later, however, when I put on a British record, the same sound distortion resulted. It was the British radiogram and not the Soviet record that was at fault. I felt I had been taught a lesson about prejudice.

At this time I succeeded in getting an article explaining our policy on exchanges into the Soviet *Literary Gazette*. It was almost unprecedented at this time for a Western spokesman to have a letter with non-Marxist political overtones published in a Moscow newspaper. The Times's Moscow correspondent declared that it contained 'some of the most outspoken criticisms by a foreigner ever seen in the Soviet press'. This gave an exaggerated impression. However, after criticizing Soviet restrictions on free contact and restating British policy in familiar terms, I added some profoundly non-Marxist statements.

The Moscow Literary Gazette published the article fully and accurately, accompanying it with a reply from a senior cultural official, Mr V. Yakovlev, who did not challenge the principles laid down in my article, but put appropriate glosses on them: Soviet facts about British unemployment and destitution were taken from British newspapers; the language of ideology was certainly the language of dissension 'when the "Voice of America" slandered Soviet institutions which millions of Soviet citizens respected; many more Soviet citizens would come as tourists to Britain if British trade policy enabled the Soviet Union to earn more sterling.'

The committee's first year had been successful. We had achieved a marked increase in contacts of all kinds with the Russians, a large and growing proportion of them through the representative British organizations. But then, in November 1956, the Soviet army launched its brutal invasion of Hungary. A wave of indignation swept over the country. Even if we had wished to – and none of us did – we had no alternative but to suspend operations.

There was an immediate problem: the Sadler's Wells Ballet, with the SRC's support, was due to pay a much-heralded visit to Moscow. The first night would have been a major diplomatic occasion, attended by the Soviet leaders and ambassadors of many countries. While the arrests and executions continued in Hungary, this was unthinkable. We had no alternative but to cancel the visit.

Inevitably, this gave the long-looked-for opening for the left-wingers to attack the SRC. The tone was set soon after by the Russians in an article in the Moscow Literary Gazette by M. Vilensky:

It is a sad paradox, but it is a fact, that the Chairman of the Committee dealing with Cultural Relations with the USSR is a convinced antagonist of such relations. Alas, he seems actively to antagonize the English people against the Soviet Union. He makes the relations between the two countries more difficult by all means at his disposal. This does not only refer to his articles. It is well-known that the Committee headed by Mayhew has stopped the journey of the Sadler's Wells Ballet troupe to Moscow. The refusal was motivated by events in Hungary. Mr Mayhew's hand-writing may be recognized without difficulty.

This means that counter revolutionaries should be permitted to settle their accounts with patriots, that followers of Horthy should be allowed to trample with their jackboots on innocent people; that they should be permitted to burn some alive and to hang by their legs other people. Do not stop the bandits and then, only then, will Christopher Mayhew graciously permit the fairies from Covent Garden to shine with their mastery on the Moscow stage.

The line of Mr Mayhew's behaviour, which goes across the channels of Anglo-Soviet cultural relations, is causing blame in England itself. The Deputy-Chairman of the National Executive Committee of the Labour Party, Tom Driberg, referred to the decision to cancel the journey to Moscow of the English Ballet troupe as 'idiotic and regrettable'. In the newspaper Reynold's News Driberg gives an expanded characteristic of the activities of the Committee, headed by Mayhew. This is what he writes: 'The object of the Committee, of which Mayhew is the Chairman, consists of the improvement in Anglo-Soviet relations. If this Committee sincerely aims at realizing this target, then it must agree that mutual Anglo-Soviet understanding, in spite of all drawbacks, remains the main hope for peace in the whole world. This mutual understanding should continue, in order to improve relations when, and especially if, they are at their worst. Otherwise this Committee appears only as a tool of the external policy of the British government, and, if the government will renew the cold war, then this Committee may just as well cease to exist.' In this evaluation there is quite a lot of justice.

Reynolds News was the only left-wing Sunday newspaper and Driberg's weekly articles were very influential with Labour Party activists. His attack on me was headlined 'Come off it Chris!' He commented that out of a record numbers of letters he had received about the cancellation of the Sadler's Wells visit, only four supported it. 'One was a pro-Eden Tory, another, unfortunately a patient in a mental hospital. Another is Christopher Mayhew MP.'

I disliked and distrusted Driberg. He had just returned from a visit to Moscow where, with special permission from the KGB, he had interviewed Guy Burgess for some newspaper articles and a book. These whitewashed Burgess, who was an old friend of Driberg's.

In my reply in *Reynold's News*, after explaining the reasons for the cancellation, I raised this point. 'I am often disturbed at Driberg's apparent reluctance in his *Reynold's* articles to criticize communists, whether British or Russian. A good example is his attitude to Burgess ('Guy'). Burgess was a communist – a Stalinist – who deceived and betrayed the Labour movement (especially our good comrade Hector McNeil), and he deserves much rougher treatment than he gets from Driberg who is, after all, Vice Chairman of the Labour Party.' Driberg replied:

Mayhew's reference to Guy Burgess is an example of prejudice in the strict sense of the word. . . . If he wants to know what my attitude really is (but I suspect he doesn't) it may be summed up thus: I do not think Burgess was a 'traitor' or a Soviet agent; I do not agree with his action in going to Russia.

To this I replied, 'I knew Burgess when he was at the Foreign Office. The best commentary on his politics and personality is the simple fact – which I invite Driberg to deny – that he left Attlee's Britain secretly and in haste, and in very bad company, to take up residence in Stalin's Russia with the permission of Beria.'

In spite of the Russians' bitter attacks on the SRC over Hungary, it was common ground between us that the programme of exchanges ought to be resumed as soon as this became practicable.

For our part, although we had no means of measuring the impact of our exchanges on Soviet opinion, it was reasonable to assume that they were positive from our point of view, and we had certainly succeeded in devaluing the efforts of the British communists in this field. For its part, the Soviet government was undoubtedly under pressure from its intelligentsia to widen its contacts with the West and, though Hungary had increased its reliance on the BSFS and SCR, it was aware of the limitations of these organizations.

On 15 January 1957, a senior Soviet embassy official, Mr Bogatyrev, wrote a reproachful but polite letter to *The Times*, and I replied:

... like everyone else, we ourselves have been badly shaken by events in Hungary. When we formed the Committee two years ago, we hoped that the Soviet regime was sincerely trying to shake off its Stalinist past, and normalize relations with the West, and we thought that the peoples of the West should respond in a friendly and constructive manner. We still hope that normalization is the long-term policy of the Soviet regime; and, as this becomes clearer, we look forward to resuming our former collaboration with the Soviet embassy and Ministry of Culture.

But our friends must know that the extent to which the Soviet government persists in actions such as those it took in Hungary, to that extent the work of the Soviet Relations Committee, and, indeed the whole course of British–Soviet friendship, is made impossible.

In fact, the SRC was already discussing with the Foreign Office ways and means of resuming our programme of exchanges, and on 23 February 1957 the Foreign Secretary sent us a formal statement approving the resumption of contacts, and asking us to draw up the programme of exchanges for 1957/8. He stated that for the time being contacts should concentrate on 'unpretentious' exchanges, especially of students, and should avoid large-scale manifestations. This was in line with our committee's views. Other suggestions by the Secretary of State seemed to us unrealistic, and since the SRC was a voluntary, non-official body, we felt free to ignore them.

In 1957 I visited Moscow with a delegation to work out a plan of exchanges for 1958/9. It was quickly and amicably concluded. However, I suffered one moment of fearful embarrassment. Our delegation included Sir Arthur Bliss, Master of the Queen's Music, Sir Philip Hendy, Director of the British Museum and Sir Paul Sinker, Director-General of the British Council. We had just signed our agreement with the Russians on a programme of cultural exchanges and, after a magnificent banquet, they had transported us to the front row of the stalls at the Bolshoi, for a performance of *Figaro*.

Music lovers will agree that the plot of this incomparable opera is complicated enough even for those who can understand the language in which it is sung, and who have not been stupefied by food, drink and long hours of negotiating with Russians. So, when the curtain came down, to a storm of cheers, on the famous ensemble in Act 3, I signalled to my colleagues and we stood up and started moving towards the exit. But then, halfway up the aisle, I noticed people still sitting down and looking at us strangely. The dreadful truth dawned: there is a fourth act in *Figaro*.

What was to be done? Could we pretend that we were tired, or ill, or had another engagement? No, we couldn't. There was nothing for it. I turned round. 'Back we go. Sorry!' I whispered, and to widespread Soviet titters the cream of British culture about-turned and slunk back into their seats.

On my return from Moscow I found a letter from Charles Hill, the newly appointed Minister of Information, inviting me to tell him how the government could help the work of the SRC. After explaining the committee's work in some detail, I made some suggestions:

In relation to the Communist Front organizations in this country, I think it is necessary to work out and pursue a calculated policy of breaking them. We were in sight of victory in the autumn of 1956, when the Soviet Relations Committee had established a sufficiently powerful position in the field of cultural exchanges to make it very difficult for the Russians to deal with the societies. Unfortunately, since Hungary, this position has been lost. In my view the following action is necessary. First, we must restore the Committee to its previous standing by an expansion of its activities in all fields (we are now doing this). Then we must explain to the British public the full story of the manner in which communists and fellow-travellers are obstructing the proper development of cultural relations between the two countries, and point out the harm done to British–Soviet relations by the British Soviet Friendship Society and the Society for Cultural Relations. Finally, the British government must cause the complete failure of a major communist-sponsored visit of Russian artists to this country by delaying a sufficient proportion of visas for a sufficiently long period of time. This will involve the societies and the impresarios who deal with them in a loss of money and prestige which might well prove disastrous to them. A good time for doing this might be next autumn, when the annual celebrations of the October Revolution come round, and the British–Soviet Friendship Society, backed by the Soviet embassy in London, organizes its 'Friendship Month' and greets streams of Soviet artists etc. coming to this country.

As explained earlier, the main priority of the Soviet Relations Committee is freeing contacts between the masses of people, and within this objective we give special attention to youth and student exchanges. This is certainly the most important aspect of the whole question of British–Soviet cultural relations. By taking the initiative, the Russians were able to attract over 1500 students and youths from Britain this year to their Moscow Festival. The organization in Britain, the British Youth Festival Committee, was wholly communist controlled, and in addition the festival was sponsored internationally by the two communist youth organizations, the World Federation of Democratic Youth (WFDY) and the International Union of Students (IUS). (This means that even if the British contingent had been properly chosen and organized, it would have been out-voted on all organizational questions by a combination of communists from communist countries and communists from non-communist countries.)

It is essential for the Western governments to work out a clear, positive answer to this communist challenge in the field of youth contacts. I have myself made suggestions from time to time to the Foreign Office that we should propose the holding of properly organized East–West international youth festivals, either under the auspices of the United Nations, or by agreement between the Communist International youth organizations and the non-Communist International youth organization, the World Assembly of Youth. Unfortunately, these ideas have not been taken up. If nothing is done, the Western countries will be in a new and still more difficult dilemma by 1961, when the next Communist International Youth Festival is launched.

Meantime the Committee has forestalled one of the worst effects of the Moscow Youth Festival – the inviting back of Soviet students and youth to this country by British Communist youth organizations – by itself issuing an invitation to 300 Soviet students and youths in the name of all the respectable youth organizations in the country. This has put the Russians in a difficult position. They have accepted our invitation to send over representatives for discussions, and this will make it difficult (though by no means impossible) for them to do business with the communists in the field. I think this shows the importance of the main point I wish to emphasize – that the problem of British–Soviet exchanges can only be tackled successfully if we constantly keep the initiative. And for this, strong, imaginative backing is required from the government.[2]

What action, if any, Charles Hill took as a result of this appeal I have no means of knowing. However, shortly afterwards the budget of the Committee was raised to £100,000 a year.

The issue of youth exchanges was highly contentious at this time, and I found myself under fire from the left for opposing British participation in communist-organized youth festivals. In a letter to *The Times* of 18 August 1959, I urged that the expansion of youth exchanges should be organized on a 'coexistence' basis – that is between representative (communist) youth in the East and representative (non-communist) youth in the West and not on the old cold war basis between communists in the East and West. A few days later, an editorial in the Soviet youth paper *Komsomolskaya Pravda* declared that: 'In a tirade betraying his annoyance and anger, Mr Mayhew lectured the young Britons that they had done wrong by going to the festival. ... Mr Mayhew's latest attack on the wonderful Vienna Festival can only be resented by Soviet young people and anyone who values peace and friendship between the nations.'

Surprisingly, the SRC had an enemy on the 'right', the *Daily Express*. Its proprietor, Lord Beaverbrook, had been conducting a personal vendetta against the British Council for most of his active life. A leading article in the *Daily Express* read:

The do-gooders have a new mania – swapping 'good will' with the Russians. ... Mr Christopher Mayhew is asking for more money to spend on 'cultural relations'. He is chairman of a British Council committee that wants to send British musicians, dancers and films to Russia.

No less than £30,000 of public money is allotted to this nonsensical committee. And now Mr Mayhew and his colleagues demand a further contribution of £38,000. Is it not a scandal? The country is clamped in a credit squeeze, but the culture-and-cocktail set get public money for Iron Curtain junkets. It should be stopped.

However, the work of the Soviet Relations Committee was less simple than this, as a report of mine to the Foreign office showed:

I lunched with Malik, the Soviet Ambassador, yesterday. I was surprised that the only other guest was Gromeka (the General Secretary of the Soviet organization which promoted Friendship societies worldwide) who was over here under BSFS auspices, despite our objections.

Mr Malik talked in a most controversial manner throughout, and I had the feeling that he wanted to draw me out and display me to Gromeka as impossibly anti-communist and anti-Soviet. I tried to be patient, but it was hard, especially since I had not wished to meet Gromeka.

I asked Gromeka about his present visit. He said that he was meeting 'more people' than on his two previous visits when he came under the auspices of the National Union of Teachers. He said he naturally did not ask people he met whether they were communist, but he was sure many weren't. I asked him what organizations he had contacted. He read out from his notebook with an air of triumph, 'The Nottingham Co-operative Society, the Lord Mayor of Coventry, the Coventry Trades Council, the Leicester Co-operative Society, the Royal Photographic Society, and the Royal Geographic Society.' When I asked about artists and writers, he replied with satisfaction that he was due to visit the Association of Folk Dancers the following day.

I stated that Gromeka's visit under the auspices of the BSFS and SCR was unwelcome and could do nothing but harm in the long run to British–Soviet relations.

Malik then said – as he had said before – that the Society for Cultural Relations should be made more representative, and Gromeka put in that many members of BSFS had said to him that they would welcome Labour Party members and resented that the BSFS was proscribed by Transport House: 'Those who split the working class movement (sic) carried a heavy responsibility.'

The Cultural Cold War

I explained that ordinary British people did not wish to join communist organizations, especially when recommended to do so by Russians: nor did the Labour Party with six million members wish to cooperate in any way with a dwindling, ageing and discredited party of 27,000.
Malik here remarked half humorously that we could always suppress such Societies. I explained that we believed in allowing complete freedom to our communists and would do nothing of the kind; but it was felt that advantage was being taken of our tolerance.
As we were leaving they both pressed me very strongly on the point of visiting Moscow. I explained that the Committee's attitude on this point was also influenced by financial considerations. We had applied for a larger budget and must hope that our application would be successful.[3]

This Moscow visit went ahead from 24 to 28 March 1959. As chairman of the British delegation, I was accompanied by Sir Fitzroy Maclean, who was acting vice-chairman of our committee, Dr R. S. Aitken, chairman of the Committee of Vice-Chancellors and Principals of the Universities of the United Kingdom, and also Sir Paul Sinker. The negotiations were formal, but quite friendly, and laid down a programme of exchanges for 1959 and the first quarter of 1960. The communiqué announced that the next meeting of the two sides would take place in London in 1959 to agree a programme of exchanges for 1960/1.

An article in the *Economist* of 11 April 1959 praised the work of 'the cold warriors of the Soviet Relations Committee of the British Council' and said 'The iron curtain has still very few holes. Many years of patient work lie ahead of the British Council; its importance can scarcely be over-estimated. However, I was feeling increasingly that the role of the Soviet Relations Committee had now become anomalous, and that a new set-up for organizing exchanges was needed. On 14 March 1959, I wrote to David Ormsby Gore (later Lord Harlech), the junior Foreign Office minister in charge of information matters.

I pointed out that while the SRC had been glad to negotiate the first British–Soviet cultural agreements with the Soviet government, this was not an appropriate role for a non-official body – let alone for an opposition MP. The Russians wanted future negotiations to be on an inter-governmental basis, and they were right.

At the same time, for administrative and security reasons, the SRC was unable to fulfil the much-needed function of bringing together in a single body all the organizations and individuals engaged in exchanges with the Soviet Union, so as to encourage and guide their efforts and give the final *coup de grâce* to the front organizations. I recommended that a Foreign Office committee with British Council representation should take over the conduct of negotiations with the Soviet Union, and that a new unofficial organization, proof against communist infiltration, should bring together unofficial organizations involved in British–Soviet exchanges.

These suggestions were approved by the Foreign Office, who obtained a modest subsidy from the Treasury for a new unofficial body.

With the help of Fitzroy Maclean MP and Gilbert Longden MP, I had already drafted a constitution for the new organization, and in due course a very well attended meeting was held under the chairmanship of Fitzroy Maclean, and the new organization, the Great Britain–USSR Association was born. I persuaded Attlee, without any difficulty, to become its president. In due course this developed into today's high-powered and well-endowed British–Russian Centre and British–East/West Centre.

I think all the members of the Soviet Relations Committee felt sad when we came to recommend our own winding up. We had worked well together. With my successive Conservative vice-chairmen – Sir Charles Mott-Radclyffe MP, Sir Gilbert Longden MP and Sir Fitzroy Maclean MP – I had a very happy relationship. Fitzroy Maclean was particularly helpful during the 1959 negotiations in Moscow, thanks to his great knowledge of the Soviet peoples and his perfect command of Russian.

The SRC also owed a great deal to the British Council's director-general, Sir Paul Sinker, who coped with all our administrative problems, calling on the considerable resources of the British Council as necessary. A robust and forthright character, he had little liking for the Soviet bureaucrats with whom we had to deal. On one occasion when we were engaged in a serious discussion in the Soviet embassy, he exclaimed abruptly to Ambassador Malik, 'The trouble is, nobody believes a word you say!' I had some difficulty in getting him to apologize, and in calming down the Ambassador, who, reasonably enough, was threatening to leave the room.

The trade union representatives on the committee – first Sir Vincent Tewson and then Sir Victor Feather – seldom attended our meetings. But having them as members increased our democratic credentials and may have impressed the Russians.

Regular attenders at our meetings were the successive heads of the northern department of the Foreign Office. They were our link with the Moscow embassy and, when necessary, with Foreign Office ministers. They also interceded for us occasionally with the Treasury. However, they were careful to respect the SRC's independent status and seldom opposed our decisions.

A senior British Council official, Miss Brenda Tripp, was the committee's secretary, and handled our affairs admirably.

During my time with the SRC, I naturally had many meetings with eminent Soviet artists and intellectuals. I was always discreet. Why embarrass them? I knew they would have been warned against me.

In his memoirs, Dmitri Shostakovich rails against the Western journalists he met. 'Every one of these pushy fellows wants me to answer his stupid questions "daringly" and these gentlemen take offence when they don't hear what they want. Why do I have to answer? Why do I have to risk my life?'[4]

I knew that my guests wouldn't give themselves away for an instant. They wouldn't trust me, and quite right too. But all the time they were saying 'keep it up. This is what we want – to go abroad, to get away from Marxism, to see the outside world for ourselves.'

The SRC's work had not been without its annoyances and embarrassments. There was, for example, the bizarre welcome we gave to the Bolshoi Ballet in 1955. At a late date, the British government had laid it down that the Soviet jet aircraft was too noisy to be allowed to land at Heathrow. This caused considerable inconvenience and led to some warm protests from Moscow and from Ambassador Malik. I protested myself, but without success. So, in due course, the reception committee made its tortuous way through the rain to Stanstead airport, where the small and rather sleazy reception room soon filled with distinguished and indignant British actors, led by Paul Scofield. I managed to find a seat for the Ambassador, who made no effort to hide his extreme displeasure with the organizers of the reception, myself included. The situation would have been trying enough if the plane had arrived punctually, but in fact it was more than two hours late; and when it did arrive, when Paul Scofield and his glamorous friends had run towards it over the tarmac, waving flowers, it was discovered that the exit door of the aircraft was a great deal higher than the landing platform offered by Stanstead airport. So there we stood on the tarmac, smiling up and waving ineffectually, until, after an interminable delay, a ladder was improvised.

There was also a brief but anxious moment when the Bolshoi Ballet visited Stratford-on-Avon. Our special train drew up carefully, so that the door of Galina Ulanova's carriage stopped at the red carpet on the platform, opposite the Mayor and Town Clerk, in their ceremonial attire, and a small group of onlookers. Ulanova stepped out with a smile. The (lady) Mayor moved forward and then suddenly stopped, looking down. Her feet were encircled by a wayward and impudent black silk slip. However, to everyone's relief, her escort promptly picked it up and put it in his pocket. Neither lady batted an eyelid and proceeded serenely with the welcoming ceremony.

Ulanova endeared herself to everyone. Not so Madame Furtseva, Mikhailov's successor as Soviet minister of culture, who absented herself without warning or explanation from a dinner arranged in her honour by the Soviet Relations Committee. This was thought to be because her host was not a minister but merely myself. She was a tall, bosomy, bureaucratic lady and I disliked her very much.

Equally contemptuous of the committee and of myself was the newspaper tycoon and fraudster Robert Maxwell. In 1954 he came up to me at a Labour Party conference – we were then fellow Labour MPs – to tell me that he had just returned from Moscow where he had found I was unpopular with leading cultural officials. He explained that they were quite easy to get on with and that he had successfully negotiated with them a big contract for the sale of Soviet books in the Western world, including the Soviet encyclopaedia.

We now know that Maxwell was then a good friend of the chief of the KGB, Vladimir Kryuchkov, and that his arrangements in Moscow had been made by the KGB.[5] At the time I was unaware of this: it seemed only natural that the Soviet cultural bureaucracy should give a warm welcome to someone willing and able to give a powerful boost to their propaganda in Western countries.

Some 35 years later, the government began an enquiry into the dealings of Maxwell's firm, Pergamon, with the Soviet Union. I wrote to the Foreign Secretary, Douglas Hurd: 'I think at that time he was simply acting as an enterprising and unprincipled businessman, but later slipped – perhaps without fully realizing it – into the role of the well-rewarded propaganda agent.' Douglas Hurd replied: 'Robert Maxwell of course kept close contacts with the old East European and Soviet leaderships. They are not the company you or I would have chosen; but *de mortuis nil nisi bonum* – or at least, up to a point.'

I was disappointed by the SRC's inability to arrange contacts between British and Soviet Jews. As I explained in a letter to Barnett Janner MP (later Lord Janner):

I have had a few words with the Chargé d'Affaires, Mr Roschin, whom I have always found to be responsible and sensible on past occasions. Unfortunately I have to tell you that his reactions were not promising. He stated that people of Jewish faith in the Soviet Union did not regard themselves as a separate community and were not anxious for contacts with their coreligionists abroad. ... This reaction is, I am bound to say, very much what I would have expected. ... There is, of course, no difficulty whatever in British citizens of Jewish faith visiting the Soviet Union, and I have no doubt that they would meet some of their coreligionists in the ordinary course of foreign travel. But it seems fairly clear to me that the Soviet authorities are unwilling to give any kind of encouragement to British–Soviet contacts along the lines you hoped for.[6]

In 1960, Hugh Gaitskell, under increasing attack from unilateralists and leftists, asked me to spend more time helping the party in parliament. He had some right to ask for this. For the previous ten years, besides my non-party involvement in British–Soviet relations, I had been producing and presenting regular documentaries on current affairs for BBC television, and writing weekly articles for the *Star*.

Besides terminating my BBC contract, I decided to spend less time on British–Soviet relations.

However, there were still two initiatives in this field that seemed worthwhile. The first was to extend the British Council's involvement in the Soviet Union to the communist countries in eastern Europe. In October 1962 I made this proposal to the Foreign Secretary, Sir Alec Douglas-Home (later Lord Home). The idea was approved and in due course the executive committee of the British Council established the East Europe Committee, appointing myself as chairman and Gilbert Longden MP as vice-chairman.

This new post took little of my time, since our work was much more straightforward than the work of the old Soviet Relations Committee had been. All the east European governments keenly supported the committee and gave little or no encouragement to their 'friendship' organizations. Many fruitful new contacts of all kinds were arranged. This was not a cold war operation, but rather a much-needed extension of the routine work of the British Council.

The second initiative was an attempt to persuade other European countries to follow Britain's example in their contacts with the communist states. At this time I was a British delegate to the Council of Europe and rapporteur of the Committee of Non-Represented (namely communist) Countries. I wrote a report recommending a major extension of contacts with communist countries on a representative basis, and this was accepted by the Council without serious opposition. The Assembly recommended, among other things, 'That the Committee of Ministers should initiate contacts of many kinds, including fellowships and scholarships for scientists, artists and scholars, with these countries on a multilateral basis under the auspices of the Council of Europe.' The resolution was accepted on 9 May 1963.

At the beginning, my interest in creating contacts with the Soviet Union had been entirely political. I had wanted to do something to weaken Soviet misconceptions about the West. But as time had gone on, as I made the acquaintance of leading British and Soviet actors, writers and musicians, my motivation began to change. I saw how easily great music, drama and literature leap national and ideological frontiers. On one occasion I witnessed a British audience acclaiming with genuine enthusiasm a performance of *The Cherry Orchard* by the Moscow State Theatre in *Russian*. On that occasion, in a speech of thanks backstage I said: 'How can an English audience respond so warmly to a play in Russian? It is because Chekhov and Shakespeare speak the same language. It is because great drama, literature, art and music reflect values which hold good for all peoples at all times.'

These profoundly non-Marxist sentiments plainly stirred the Russians. I think they felt, as I myself did increasingly, that the true value of cultural exchanges was not for bringing people together, or for displaying goodwill or for promoting an ideology. First and foremost, *The Cherry Orchard* and *Hamlet*, Britten's War Requiem and Shostakovich's Fifth Symphony were forces for peace because of the magic in them. To use them for political purposes, however fruitfully, was to diminish them.

Chapter 4
Against 'Peace'

Opposing the Soviet idea of 'friendship' had been a congenial and rewarding experience: opposing their idea of 'peace' was a much tougher affair. It was an article of Marxist faith that the primary cause of war was capitalism. It followed that the struggle for peace was the struggle against the 'capitalist camp' – against US imperialism, the Atlantic Pact, German rearmament, Western colonial rule, the economic recovery of western Europe and, above all, US and British nuclear weapons.

In 1949, Stalin founded the World Peace Council, to bring together communists and non-communists of all countries in a united struggle for this Marxist concept of 'peace'. Its first manifestation in Britain was the Sheffield Peace Congress held in 1950. To coincide with its opening, I wrote an article for the *Sheffield Telegraph*:

The Sheffield Congress is the last place for peace lovers to find themselves. It is not concerned with peace at all. We get a clue to its real purpose by studying the records of the small group of communists and fellow travellers who direct it. These include people who urge the Greek guerrillas to fight their elected government; who urge the Malayan bandits to attack our troops and murder our civilians; who justify the aggression of North Korea against South Korea. They are surely the most bloodthirsty peace lovers in history. The campaigns which they support have only one thing in common. Common to them all is the fact, that, if successful, they would increase the power of the Soviet Union relative to the power of the free world.

It is useful to remember that when these communists talk of the 'fight for peace' they mean 'the fight against the war-mongers' – and by 'war-mongers' they mean you and me and the government we elect. For example the President of the British 'peace' committee, Mr J. G. Crowther,

Against 'Peace'

said in Moscow on the 18th October this year: 'Today we see how the peoples of Malaya, Vietnam and Korea are fighting for peace.' By 'the peoples' Mr Crowther meant the communist forces. By 'fighting' he meant waging war, by 'peace' he meant a communist victory. Stripped of the 'double meanings' this sentence thus reads: 'Today we see how communists in Malaya, Vietnam and Korea are waging war for communism.' Mr Crowther now comes to Sheffield to urge that peoples all over the world should follow the example of these warriors.

Though hampered by the IRD's advance publicity, the worldwide Soviet 'peace' campaign was a major source of strength to Soviet foreign policy in the 1950s and 1960s. Carried forward by the World Peace Council and by a network of other communist-led front organizations, such as the World Federation of Trade Unions, the World Federation of Democratic Youth, Scientists for Peace, Doctors for Peace and so on, it attracted support from a wide range of well intentioned non-communist 'delegates'. All the meetings were subject to communist control, skilfully obscured by the trappings of representativeness and democracy. These were the techniques with which I had become familiar 20 years earlier, as a hapless 'delegate' to the International Conference against Fascism and War in Brussels.

When the General Secretary of the World Peace Council invited me to a conference in Helsinki, I replied:

I appreciate the courteous tone of your letter and the accompanying brochure. But I also happened to read the prospectus of your conference published in a recent issue of the Cominform Journal. *Addressed mainly to communists, this made no attempt to conceal the real purpose of the conference, which is plainly to forward Soviet foreign policy and arouse prejudice against the US government. Moreover the tone of the* Cominform Journal *was as tendentious and offensive as your letter was non-committal and polite. The whole comparison seems to me a distressing example of the communist use of respectable-sounding 'front' organizations.*

It seemed to me that Britain's communists were too weak to make much impact with their own 'peace' campaigning, but that they became a major influence in Britain's most important peace organization, the Campaign for Nuclear Disarmament (CND).

British unilateralists were united in opposing British nuclear weapons. Many objected to them on moral grounds, others because they could never be used without inviting devastating retaliation, others because they encouraged nuclear proliferation, others because, by renouncing them, Britain would set an example to other countries. But all unilateralists were agreed that the British bomb should be banned and, furthermore, that American nuclear weapons should be removed from British soil.

This appeal made a big impact, not least in the Labour movement. In due course the all-powerful Transport and General Workers' Union, whose left-wing general secretary, Frank Cousins, was a leader of CND, declared for unilateralism, and successfully pushed a unilateralist motion through the Labour Party's Scarborough conference in 1960, against the fervent opposition of the leader of the party, Hugh Gaitskell.

It was after this defeat that Gaitskell appealed on the platform to his supporters to 'fight, fight and fight again' to suppress disloyal leftist elements in the party and to reverse the Scarborough decision.

We needed no encouragement and, for 12 months, conducted an intensive, bitter and ultimately victorious campaign against unilateralism and the Labour left. We were led by the Campaign for Democratic Socialism (CDS), organized in brilliant fashion by Bill Rogers MP.

Besides supporting the CDS, I made a minor contribution by forming a much smaller, specialist socialist Campaign for Multilateral Disarmament (CMD). Our aim was to present a positive alternative to unilateralism, so as to assist the reversal of the Scarborough decision, and also to impress on the Labour Party that the leading opponents of unilateralism were also active campaigners for disarmament and peace.

Our declared supporters included Philip Noel-Baker MP (a winner of the Nobel peace prize), Denis Healey MP, Douglas Jay MP, James Callaghan MP, George Brown MP and many other leading Labour personalities. Time was short, and we decided not to attempt to build up a membership. I drafted a manifesto, which was quickly approved.

We believe that peace is the supreme need of mankind. We wish for friendship with the governments and peoples of all countries.

Against 'Peace'

We are also realists. We believe that pacifism and appeasement in Britain helped to precipitate the last war, and in present circumstances could help to cause a final disastrous nuclear conflict.

Arms can sometimes prevent aggression. If the Israelis disarmed unilaterally they would be massacred by the Arabs. If the Chinese communists disarmed unilaterally, Chiang Kai-shek would march into Peking. Only British arms, and a readiness to use them, keep Franco out of Gibraltar.

If the Soviet Union disarmed unilaterally, irresistible demands would grow in certain Western countries for frontier changes in eastern Europe and the liquidation of the regimes there.

If the Western powers disarmed unilaterally, Soviet communism would overwhelm West Berlin and resume its spread Westward, based on the use or threatened use of military power.

We detest all wars, all armaments, all power politics, and will do our utmost to put an end to them. But this can only be done by agreement between nations – never by unilateral surrender of power by any one of them.

We therefore support the demands set out in Labour's declarations Foreign Policy and Defence and The Next Step for an agreement on nuclear tests, for disengagement in Europe, for reform of Nato, and in particular for stage-by-stage multilateral disarmament....

Our views, we believe, are shared by an overwhelming majority of Labour Party members. But recently they have been submerged by the propaganda – usually vigorous and sincere – of a small minority of pacifists and unilateralists, after receiving unasked-for support from very questionable sources. We have been disturbed by the disproportionate influence of these small groups inside the movement, and also by the excessive readiness of some Labour leaders to compromise with them.

We therefore intend to campaign for an acceptance by all sections of the Labour movement of the principles of all-round comprehensive disarmament and collective security on which Labour Foreign Policy, under such leaders as Arthur Henderson, Ernest Bevin and Clement Attlee, has always been based.

The CMD announced its existence by holding what we called a Multilateral Marathon at Central Hall, Westminster. For five successive days, from 5.30 p.m. onwards, teams of speakers expounded the arguments in the Manifesto and answered questions.

By normal standards the Marathon was a failure. The audiences were small; speakers often failed to turn up on time. But the novelty of the idea won publicity for the fact of our existence, which was its main objective. Our campaign also presented the unilateralists with a problem. Everyone agreed that multilateral disarmament was desirable. But could they call themselves multilateralists as well as unilateralists? I had a lively exchange on this question in *Encounter*, in March 1961, with Bertrand Russell:

CND is profoundly defeatist about the prospect of multilateral disarmament. True, some of its less logical supporters declare themselves multilateralists as well as unilateralists (as though a government could negotiate about nuclear weapons, and also abandon them, at one and the same time!) But if they really believed in the prospects of all-round multilateral disarmament, they would never have become unilateralists in the first place. CND thrives on, and fosters, the belief that multilateral disarmament discussions will never succeed.

Russell wrote:

Mr Mayhew considers it illogical to be both a unilateralist and a multilateralist. That arises only from his wilfully or ignorantly distorting the claims of those who are called unilateralists. Where is the lack of logic in saying 'we wish everybody to disarm; but, meanwhile, let us disarm ourselves?' I am, of course, willing, in all humility, to derive lessons in logic from Mr Mayhew, but, so far, my logical capacities are not equal to following his argument on this point.

To this I replied: 'In the stress of nuclear controversy, even Lord Russell's logic tends to go astray. . . . Unilateralists are those who want Britain to disarm without conditions. Multilateralists are those who want her to disarm only if other countries do the same. The two groups are thus by definition mutually exclusive.'

Inside the Labour Party the controversy became acrimonious.

Against 'Peace'

Kingsley Martin, a leading unilateralist and editor of the *New Statesman and Nation*, wrote to me on 6 February 1961.

I know that you had sunk pretty low in your argument that unilateralism was an alternative and not a means towards disarmament, but I had not guessed until reading your letter in this week's New Statesman *that you had not taken the trouble to look at the policy of CND which you have been traducing ... you should tell Dalton, Strachey and all the rest that they should read our policy statements before they misrepresent them. ...*

I can only conclude that the CMD exists to score points against the CND and is not interested in the subject. ... I can't refrain from saying that it is despicable to me that you should tell lies about your political friends – or would-be friends – for internal party reasons on a matter in which there should not be, amongst sensible people, an irreconcilable quarrel.

I also made an enemy of the retiring chairman of the Labour Party, Tony Greenwood MP, challenging him to reconcile his chairmanship of the party with his sponsoring of the current CND Manifesto, which directly opposed the party's defence policy.

I then clashed with the party's incoming chairman, Dick Crossman. He had signed an Early Day motion which opposed nuclear weapons in terms unacceptable to Hugh Gaitskell. The motion had been put down by Michael Foot and was supported by more than 50 Labour MPs. I wrote to Crossman on 6 December 1960:

I was most surprised to see that, though Chairman of the Party, you signed Michael Foot's resolution on nuclear strategy, which is so plainly aimed against the Party's parliamentary leadership. As you may have seen, with 75 other colleagues, I have put down an amendment to the motion. ... May I take it that you support this amendment and add your name to it, thus helping to forward the unity of the Party?

Crossman replied on 8 December 1960:

As you may have seen from the Order Paper, I have no objection to the words you have attached, provided we spell out their implications in a way that, unfortunately, our official defence spokesmen have lamentably failed in the past to do. Hence my addition to your addition.

By the way, if you were surprised to see my name attached to the Motion on Nuclear Strategy, I was equally surprised at your astonishing statement that this resolution 'is plainly aimed against the Party's parliamentary leadership'. Let me assure you that its only purpose was to suggest a basis for reconciliation.

However, its purpose was indeed aimed to undermine Gaitskell, whom Crossman was trying to replace with Harold Wilson. On 20 October he had written to Wilson:

I think the most important lesson I draw (speaking as your old psychological warfare adviser) is that we have now thrown Hugh on the defensive on the key issue of unity. Thank God for the Tory press which has dubbed you the 'unity candidate'. I now feel that with really hard work and consistent plugging of the unity line we can and should achieve a positive result that even you in one of your optimistic moods never calculated.[1]

With the chairman of CND, Canon John Collins, my personal relations were less stressful. In 1961, following a visit to Russia, where he had met Madame Furtseva, he asked me to lunch to discuss British–Soviet cultural relations. But the conversation soon turned to the subject of communist influence in the CND. Afterwards we exchanged letters about it:

25 July 1961
Dear John,
I thoroughly enjoyed our lunch, and was relieved and delighted to hear about your decision to hive off the Trotskyite and communist elements in CND. Everyone *seems to take the view that you have travelled far too far with them, and some even dispute my sincere view that you can and will break with them now.*

4 August 1961
Dear Christopher,
I think we are in danger, if we are not careful, of getting into a

Against 'Peace'

misunderstanding. . . . I do recognize that there is always a danger in such a movement as ours of an infiltration, and that already at least at certain levels in the campaign the process has begun. What I wanted you to know is that we are aware of this danger and will certainly do everything we can to see that it does not develop.

9 August 1961

Dear John,

I do hope I have not misrepresented you. I understood you to say that owing to the Direct Action Campaign and the new constitution, the communists had become a considerable embarrassment in CND; that control had been lost of a number of branches; that a showdown had become necessary; and that by the end of the year the movement would be split. When I suggested that the non-communists might not be strong enough even to split the movement, I understood you to say that in that case you would cease aiming at a mass movement and would form yourselves into a committee of intellectuals.

8 September 1961

Dear Christopher,

In my view if this process were allowed to continue unchecked a showdown would very soon become necessary... As far as Communist infiltration was concerned, I felt that there had been a greater measure of success than was wholesome and that a number of groups, particularly the youth groups, were in serious danger of coming under their control. . . . Should we be unable to halt the process which has begun and keep the Campaign free from control. . . . I would most certainly myself then consider resigning as Chairman of the Campaign.

9 September 1961

Dear John,

I believe if you had had the experience of some of us over the past twelve months in opposing unilateralism in Trades Unions, the Labour Party etc., you could not resist the conclusion that the rank and file of your Campaign is under strong Trotskyist and communist influence. I was shaken by your statement that you accepted communist support: we *multilateralists would utterly reject support from fascist forces! Lunch is on me next time.*

Soon afterwards, my friend and constituent Nicholas Stacey, Rector of Woolwich, wrote to me on 25 October 1961, 'Canon Collins was telling me that he thought you, more than any other man, had stopped the Labour Party going unilateralist. And he meant it.'

If he had indeed meant it, he was doubly wrong. Other opponents of unilateralism had done far more than I had – George Brown, Bill Rogers, Hugh Gaitskell himself, and others; and the Labour Party had not been stopped from going unilateralist. On the contrary, after Gaitskell's death, when Harold Wilson, followed by Michael Foot and James Callaghan, became party leaders, the floodgates were opened to the unilateralists, along with left-wing union bosses and the 'lunatic left', and in due course the party became officially, and disastrously, committed to a unilateralist defence policy.

In 1960, Gaitskell appointed me deputy to Harold Wilson who was Shadow Foreign Secretary ('I want you to keep an eye on Harold'). My function was to expound Labour policy and challenge government policy. However, I felt that the Marxist left provided a greater threat to the Labour Party and the country than the Conservative right, and I continued to counter Marxist and unilateralist 'peace' propaganda. 'Peaceful coexistence' – a flawed and divisive concept – presented an immediate challenge.

This slogan was not new; it had been launched in Stalin's time. But in his report to the twentieth Communist Party Congress in February 1956, Khrushchev had given the concept a powerful new emphasis, making clear that while struggle was inevitable between the communist and capitalist worlds, and that communism would prevail, revolution was not the only road to communism and armed conflict between the two camps was not inevitable.

In the non-communist world this formulation was widely taken to amount to a policy of 'live and let live', and was welcomed as such, and made a strong impact. However, for communists, its real meaning was entirely different.

Meeting in Moscow in December 1960, the world's 81 communist

Against 'Peace'

parties declared: 'Peaceful coexistence of states with differing social systems does not mean a reconciliation between socialist and bourgeois ideologies. On the contrary, it implies an intensification of the struggle of all communist parties for the triumph of socialist ideas.' And, on 6 January 1961, Khrushchev himself declared: 'The policy of peaceful coexistence is a form of intense economic, political and ideological struggle of the proletariat against the aggressive forces of imperialism in the international field.' Or, as he exclaimed on another occasion, 'We will bury you!'

This was the real Marxist concept. It was obviously divisive and provocative, obviously less likely to encourage peace than to undermine it.

I decided to try to popularize a new definition of coexistence and use this to undermine the Marxist concept. As a start, I wrote a long article in the *Guardian* on the following lines:

The Marxist concept of peaceful coexistence is based on the assumption that the social systems of the world can be realistically divided into two groups, labelled 'capitalist' and 'communist', that a 'struggle' is inevitable between so-called 'capitalist' and so-called 'communist' states; that it should be intensified, and will lead to victory of the 'communist' states – in the nuclear age, the relationship between states should be one of mutual tolerance. . . . Peace loving people should take their stand on the concept of 'coexistence plus' – plus *ideological coexistence,* plus *genuinely free East/ West contacts* – plus *practical East–West cooperation.*

As Marxists quickly saw, and as I was well aware myself, this concept amounted to a total repudiation of Marxism. At the same time, it seemed not only genuinely constructive but also likely to win far more support – especially in the Third World – than the Marxist concept of 'peaceful coexistence.'

I had sent a copy of the *Guardian* article in advance to my old friends in the Information Research Department. No doubt as a result, the day after it was published, the Minister of State at the Foreign Office, the Earl of Dundee, quoted extensively from it in the House of Lords. He declared: 'I should like to say that the government welcomes this article which corresponds with its own views.' A few days later, in a speech in Birmingham, the Foreign Secretary, Lord Home (then Sir Alec Douglas-Home) added his support. Hugh Gaitskell, leader of the opposition, also expressed support for it.

This should have been the beginning of a major campaign. I could and should have brought together a strong all-party campaign committee, made contact with like-minded foreign organizations, raised campaign funds (with the discreet help of IRD), and initiated a worldwide debate between the Western and Soviet conceptions of coexistence, which the West would certainly have won.

However, I failed to do this. Unbelievably I had simply not seen the strong statements of support from the government. Nor had anyone drawn them to my attention. I had suspected that the idea of ideological coexistence would be generally unacceptable to Conservative opinion. Was it not defeatist? Should our aim not be the destruction of communism? Were we not winning the war of ideas as things were?

Nor did I feel confident of sufficient support in my own party, riven with conflict between left and right, unilateralists and multilateralists. To test the water, I sent a copy of the *Guardian* article to Tony Benn, who replied, coolly and correctly, that it was anti-Marxist and anti-Soviet. Would it be fair to my beleaguered leader, Hugh Gaitskell, to inject this new source of discord into the Parliamentary Labour Party? For whatever reason, perhaps simply lacking the confidence of my conviction, I failed to organize a campaign, and confined myself to writing and broadcasting in support of the new idea.

What I felt sure about was that 'Coexistence Plus' would provoke alarm and anger in Moscow; and this was certainly the case. After broadcasting about it on the BBC's overseas services, I was soon engaged in a protracted and robust debate with leading Soviet ideologists.

The first to reply was Victor Mayevsky, deputy editor of *Pravda*. After a lengthy defence of the Soviet concept of coexistence, and its alleged support for freedom of contact between East and West, Mr Mayevsky declared on Moscow radio:

... and this brings us to the very crux of Christopher Mayhew's formula 'coexistence plus'. Peaceful coexistence as it is doesn't suit Mr Mayhew. He would like to add to it ideological coexistence.

Against 'Peace'

By a stroke of the pen Christopher Mayhew would do away with the laws of social development — the class struggle, national liberation and revolutionary movements. In doing so he fails to notice that he has landed himself in a ludicrous position for by rejecting the objective fact of the existence of two social systems, Mr Mayhew is himself conducting an ideological attack on the communists from a position of rabid anti-communism. In other words, while trying to prove the futility of ideological struggle, he himself acts as one of its exponents. Mr Mayhew is not in the position to abolish ideological struggle. No one is. So long as there are classes, the interests of different classes of society are bound to clash. Who can order British workers not to fight for fair pay against the Tory wage freeze, for better working conditions? Who can get an inhabitant, say of Kenya, to give up his demand for independence, or still less to work for the end of colonial oppression? No one.

My broadcast reply was distinctly disingenuous:

Why do Mr Mayevsky and his fellow Marxists insist on the necessity of ideological struggle between, for example, the Soviet Union and the United Kingdom? Are they not anxious, as we are in this country, to improve relations between our countries and increase friendship? When a demand is made by British or Soviet workers for better housing or more consumer goods or more pay, could we not agree to refrain from exploiting this as part of a propaganda battle between us?

But no, as a good Marxist, Mr Mayevsky must insist on his ideological struggle. And peace-loving people who heard his broadcast, including his criticisms of my country, will have been disappointed and disturbed by it. I am sure that in his heart he wishes to avoid nuclear war, but his methods of creating a peaceful climate are strange.

When Marxists survey the world today — a world filled with a multitude of different peoples and social systems, people with a longing for peace, friendship and unity — they feel compelled by their Marxist dogmatism to sort them out into what Mr Mayevsky calls the two opposite social systems — 'capitalism' and 'socialism' — and then to declare that struggle between the two groups is inevitable.

Today, with the great powers armed to the teeth with annihilating nuclear weapons, the Marxist conception of competitive coexistence must now give place to a more civilized conception.

In due course, Mayevsky made a second reply to this, and other speakers on Radio Moscow weighed in. I also found myself widely attacked in the Soviet press.

A year later, when I wrote a booklet *Coexistence Plus* for Bodley Head, Soviet reaction was even sharper. Vitaly Korionov made repeated attacks on me on Radio Moscow, and my brochure was further honoured by being criticized at length in *Kommunist*, the main periodical of the Central Committee of the Soviet Communist Party. Possibly Khrushchev had read this when he declared in Moscow, in March 1963, 'Ideological coexistence would be the death of Marxism.'

The Bodley Head booklet was reviewed widely and quite favourably in the British press, and 8000 copies were distributed abroad in foreign languages by IRD and the BBC. Moreover, the BBC's overseas services plugged the idea strongly. So 'coexistence plus' may have had some impact in the Third World, for which it was particularly designed. However, its impact in the West was disappointing. When I introduced the idea to the Council of Europe, as rapporteur of the relevant committee, the reaction was lukewarm. Many hard-line opponents of communism, especially in Europe and the United States, resisted the idea, assuming, naively, that it was a form of compromise with the Soviet Union. Moreover the glittering prospect of total victory in the war of ideas was already visible on the horizon.

I had started up 'coexistence plus' simply as a propaganda ploy, as a means of subverting the Soviet view of 'peaceful coexistence'. With hindsight, however, it now seems to me to have been a concept of real worth, and I wish very much that I could have succeeded in popularizing it more widely – especially in the United States.

It would have drawn attention to, and thus exacerbated, the fundamental and long-lasting contradiction in Soviet policy: the contradiction between their wish for *détente* and, with it, disarmament, and their dogmatic belief that they were duty bound to foster the growth of communism worldwide.

We know now that in the Cuban missile crisis in 1962 and the Middle

Against 'Peace'

East crisis in 1973, members of the Soviet Presidium often differed on the relative priority that should be given to these two incompatible objectives.[2] In the event, they refused to abandon either: the concept of 'coexistence plus' was rejected at the highest level for many years until Mikhail Gorbachev came to power in 1985. In 1988, he and his foreign minister, Eduard Shevardnadze, explicitly repudiated the concept of 'peaceful coexistence' proclaimed by Nikita Khrushchev and Leonid Brezhnev and the 'class basis' of international relations which had been the guiding principle of Soviet policy since Lenin's day.

It is at least arguable that if the Western governments had actively campaigned for 'coexistence plus' in the 1960s, they would have strengthened the hands of the more moderate members of the Politburo, the Marxist formulation of coexistence would have been abandoned earlier and the crises of 1962 and 1973 defused.

In 1972 I was thoroughly disillusioned with the Labour Party and seriously doubted that it could be reformed from within. Harold Wilson's tolerance of irresponsible trade union power, left-wing infiltration and unilateralism was very disturbing. Then, in 1973, the National Executive Council abolished the 'proscribed list' which had hitherto prevented Labour Party members from joining communist and fellow-travelling organizations. This was a further concession to the Marxists, and reinforced by growing conviction that the Party was beyond reform. In 1974, after an abortive attempt to replace Harold Wilson with Roy Jenkins, I left the Labour Party and joined the Liberals.[3] My press statement explained:

I have for some years been very concerned with the way the (Labour) party has been developing. In particular it has become too vulnerable to the extreme left and too dependent on the unions. Time and again in the past, moderate members, including myself, have tried to change this and to broaden the basis of the party, but with declining success, especially since Hugh Gaitskell's death. I can no longer feel genuinely convinced that a clear Labour majority at the next election will be in the country's best interest, so I have resigned.

Like other moderate Labour MPs, I have long shared many convictions with the Liberals, for example on Europe, east of Suez, industrial relations and the redistribution of wealth. But at the present time, I particularly support their campaign for political realignment. We need a revolt of the centre against the extremes.

A leader in *The Times* of 10 July 1974 perceptively commented:

Mr Mayhew's defection is symptomatic of the unease of many on the right wing of the Labour Party at this time. There will not be a stampede in parliament to join him, but a good many Labour people, as well as those of other parties, will echo his sentiments. ... Mr Mayhew has given Labour, not a body-blow, but a warning.

My change of party meant losing my seat in parliament, and it was not until 1981 when I was made a peer and the Liberal leader, David Steel, appointed me as the party's defence spokesman, that I returned to the struggle against unilateralism. This gave me an extraordinary feeling of *déjà vu*. I blew the dust off my 20-year-old speech notes and entered the fray. At this time a loose alliance had been formed between the newly-formed Social Democratic Party and the Liberals. It was particularly important for the Liberal Party to prove its multilateral credentials, otherwise it would lose the trust of its would-be partners – the Owenite Social Democrats (SDP) – in forming a centre party.

I found Liberal unilateralists no less active and enthusiastic, and a good deal less ill-natured, than their left-wing counterparts had been. But they had no leaders of the stature of Bertrand Russell or Michael Foot. On the other hand, I received less stalwart support from the Liberal leadership than I had enjoyed from Hugh Gaitskell.

At one time I felt obliged to make a reproachful protest to David Steel:

I was a bit shaken to read in The Times *today that you think Polaris should be 'cancelled'. This is the same as 'scrapped', and I thought we had agreed at that PLP meeting that 'scrapping' was simply not practicable.*

It is party policy to support NATO's strategic deterrent, of which Polaris is a part. How can we say that we support NATO's deterrent, but propose to scrap Britain's contribution to it?

Against 'Peace'

You argued at the meeting that in this case we ought to assign the subs irrevocably to NATO and renounce our right, or intention, or ability, to use them independently. This was the line taken by the incoming Wilson government in 1964 in similar circumstances, and I took it myself for a time as Navy Minister. It was very uncomfortable and unsatisfactory, but better than 'cancelling'.

Why not 'phasing out', 'not replacing', 'not renewing', 'reviewing the whole future of'? Even 'assigning irrevocably to NATO', if you must. But I do most strongly advise against 'cancelling' or 'scrapping'.[4]

Much of my time was spent trying to decide a policy on nuclear weapons acceptable to both parties. This was actually achieved by a joint Liberal–Social Democratic Defence Commission, but our unanimous declarations were promptly and publicly dismissed by David Owen as 'likely to give the British people a bellylaugh'.

Worse was to come, as the debate shifted to the issue of cruise missiles. The Soviet government had installed intermediate-range nuclear missiles in Europe to which there was no equivalent on the Western side. So should NATO respond by deploying American cruise missiles? Multilateralists said yes, unilateralists, no. The SDP said yes, the Liberals were divided.

The debate inside the Liberal Party was tense and prolonged. A unilateralist resolution had already been carried at the party's annual conference at Llandudno in 1981, and finally at our annual conference in Bournemouth, the issue was decisively concluded in favour of the unilateralists. This was very largely due to an impassioned speech against the platform by Paddy Ashdown. Naively, I had expected him to make a speech in support of the platform. But the *Guardian* commented perceptively on 21 September 1984, 'The delegates seem to have voted to phase out Mr Steel by the 1990s ... as the votes came in, the Yuppies and the Yappies squealed with delight ... the dashing young senator from Yeovil ... had just won the Bournemouth primary.' However, he had also knocked the final nail into the coffin of the Liberal-Social Democratic alliance.

A powerful weapon on the side of Liberal unilateralists had been the letters page of the Liberals' most trusted newspaper, the *Guardian*.

A War of Words

After a time, I became suspicious of its editing. Far more letters were printed from unilateralists than from multilateralists, and the headings on unilateralists' letters were notably sympathetic. Eventually, I wrote a letter of complaint to the editor, Peter Preston, who sent an unhelpful reply. It was no surprise to me when, many years later, a senior member of the *Guardian's* staff, the paper's sometime letters editor, Richard Gott, was revealed as receiving money from the KGB.

Indeed, it had seemed plain to me from the start, from the nature of their tactics and briefing, that the Liberal unilateralists were under strong communist influence. Eventually, on 22 November 1981, I wrote to the CND's director, Monsignor Bruce Kent, regretting that the CND was opposing British membership of NATO, and adding:

It is sad that CND's more moderate members seem unable to keep its communist members in better check, allowing them – to give one example – to appoint one of their own members as CND's liaison officer with the Liberal Party.

I cannot help asking whether you do not sometimes have personal qualms about helping to bring young Liberals – some of whom are very inexperienced politically – into the communist orbit in this way.

Soon afterwards, the communist in question, Dr John Cox, resigned from his post as liaison officer with Liberal CND and also from the council of CND. I publicized this welcome event, and an exchange of letters followed to the *Guardian's* editor during which Dr Cox described the work he had been doing as follows:

Each specialist section of CND, including Liberal CND, is autonomous within its chosen field, but is an integrated part of CND and calls upon CND for help in many ways (speakers, pamphlets etc.). To aid this process, we appoint liaison officers to work with each specialist section – to ensure that each receives a fair and speedy hearing for any requests for support and resources. This was the task I performed as part of my duties as CND Vice-Chairman until November 1981, I hope to the satisfaction of Liberal CND.

Against 'Peace'

Monsignor Kent defended Dr Cox and attacked me, saying that few people could have done more for CND over the years, and that Cox had just been invited to become an honorary vice-president in recognition of that work. And that they were in the business of disarmament, not of witch-hunts.

Other readers took the same line. 'Sir, if "rumbling" communists is a favourite pastime of this Lord Mayhew, then let him stick to it and leave the survival of humanity to CND. It is a pity that Monsignor Bruce Kent has wasted his valuable time on such "rumblers", for his Lordship will never replace John Cox in getting useful events on the road to peace.'[5]

The *Guardian*'s letter editor headed this correspondence 'The Cold Warrior who had burnt his fingers'.

Demands soon arose from Liberal CND for my resignation as defence spokesman, but I managed to defend myself successfully at the party council and subsequently at our 1992 annual conference.

I have said that Liberal unilateralists were better natured than their Labour equivalents. This seems to be illustrated by the following letter:

In the early 1980s, I tried to force your resignation as Liberal Defence Spokesman because I disagreed with your tough anti-CND stance. It was not (luckily) an effective campaign. I left the party in 1984 and now live and work in eastern Europe.

I am writing to say that I have realized for some time now that I was quite wrong and you were quite right. The unilateralists in the Liberal Party in the early 1980s sowed the seeds of the disastrous Eastbourne defence vote, which contributed directly to the collapse of the Alliance. More importantly, Gorbachev's reforms and arms control initiatives have demonstrated beyond doubt that the West was – and remains – quite right to maintain a strong defence and credible negotiating position. Experiencing daily life here, under the last remaining Brezhnevites, is a concrete reminder of this.

It is little comfort to be proved right by history, but it is better than being proved wrong.[6]

Chapter 5
Stalin's Foreign Friends

In the early 1960s, MI5 made an attempt to recruit me. I had known its director, Sir Roger Hollis, before the war – we were old golfing partners – and readily agreed to his request that I should meet 'two of my people'. In due course, I called at a rather splendid Georgian house north of Oxford Street, to be greeted by two friendly and confident young men. After drinks, they came to the point quickly. 'You will be well aware of the nature of our work – would you be willing to help us?' I replied that I would, that with my many Soviet contacts I thought I would be of use to them. 'Oh no!' came the reply, 'it is the Parliamentary Labour Party we are interested in.'

This surprised and annoyed me. No doubt there was a useful job to be done, helping MI5 to identify which of the 'old Labour' MPs were 'Stalin's friends'; but I could have given them the names of a dozen dependable MPs just as capable as myself of performing this task but not having my special contacts with the Soviet embassy, and in the Soviet Union.

Also, while I had no objection to spying on Soviet citizens, I felt an entirely irrational inhibition about spying on fellow members of the Parliamentary Labour Party, however deplorable their activities. Also this task would call for a talent for dissimulation which I felt would be beyond me. For all these reasons, I turned the young men down.

Altogether, though respecting MI5 from afar, I was rather disillusioned on the few occasions when I came into direct contact with it.

I have already recorded my interview with Peter Wright in 1969 when he lied to me clumsily about an invitation card MI5 had 'found' in Guy Burgess's flat. I was also annoyed when he wrote in his book, quite falsely, that I had not cooperated with him in his investigation into prewar student communism.

Stalin's Foreign Friends

There was also an incident, much earlier in 1949, which raised doubts in my mind about MI5's competence. I had been asked, as the minister responsible, to give a lecture on our anti-communist campaigning to the Imperial Defence College. The commandant of the college, Air Marshal Slessor, had assured me in advance that the audience was entirely 'secure' and that I could speak with complete freedom. However, as I was leaving after the lecture, I felt obliged to tell him that, though I felt sure his personal assistant, a staff officer, was entirely reliable, I had in fact known him before the war as a member of the Communist Party. Slessor was plainly surprised and shaken, and, in due course, an MI5 representative called on me in the Foreign Office and assured me that I had been mistaken, and that the officer in question had never been a member of the Communist Party. When he left I made two telephone calls to former communists I knew, and wrote down some details of the officer's career as a Communist Party member. I sent this to MI5 and in due course their representative reappeared to tell me that my facts were correct, that the officer concerned was now reliable – which of course I had never doubted.

Despite my disillusionment with MI5 and refusal to cooperate with them, I understood their concern about 'Stalin's foreign friends'. These existed outside as well as within the Parliamentary Labour Party.

Stalin's 'foreign friends' in Britain fell into five categories. First, the KGB agents, the spies. Next, the KGB 'agents of influence' – publicists who accepted guidance, and sometimes money, from the KGB. Then came the open Communist Party members. Then the fellow-travellers (not always easily distinguished from agents of influence). Finally, came a large class of people of the type contemptuously described by Lenin as 'useful idiots'. These people were not Party members, or consistent Marxists, but were vaguely sympathetic to the Soviet Union and engaged in activities that were helpful to the communist cause.

This classification obviously needs to be treated with caution. Stalin's friends (apart from the spies) would often move from one category to another, or, in increasing numbers, as the cold war progressed, drop out altogether. The distinction between an agent of influence and a fellow-traveller was small, as was the difference between a card-carrying communist and a communist who had been persuaded by the Party to support it without joining it.

Some of Stalin's friends I find impossible to classify. Driberg, for example. As I have mentioned earlier, I regarded him as a political (and indeed personal) adversary. He attacked me in his writings, and in the House of Commons when I was a minister. He consistently supported communist causes, was an intimate friend of Burgess and visited Moscow to interview Burgess with the assistance and goodwill of the KGB. Yet, at an earlier period of his career, he was actually recruited by MI5 and kept them informed about the executive committee of the Communist Party, of which he was a member. This practice continued until he was exposed by a fellow communist and resigned from the committee.

Driberg was thus an enigma. However, there was no difficulty about categorizing the spies. They were a class apart. My personal acquaintance with them was very limited. I do not remember meeting Burgess after I had sacked him from the IRD, or meeting Anthony Blunt after our 1935 Intourist trip to the Soviet Union. I dimly recall dining with Donald Maclean in his house in Washington, and I must at least have met Philby, because I remember in 1951 crossing the Bosphorus with our ambassador, Sir Noel Charles, to attend a party Philby gave in a handsome old house on the far shore. But, apart from Burgess, these spies seem to have made as little an impression on me as, no doubt, I did on them.

Much is made of the fact that the spies were motivated by ideology, and not by fear of blackmail or hope of financial reward. But this is surely true of the great majority of Stalin's friends in Britain. The spy Vassall responded to blackmail and John Cairncross was financially motivated. But these were the exceptions. The rest had other motivations. First, there was estrangement from capitalist society. For working-class people, capitalism created unemployment, poverty and inequality. For idealists, capitalism had no sense of direction, no spiritual aim. For ethnic minorities, it was racially prejudiced. For enemies of Nazism and fascism, it appeased Hitler and Benito Mussolini.

By contrast, the Soviet Union demonized capitalism, was hated by capitalists, had a clear-cut aim, promised change on an exhilarating scale, was self-assured and showed implacable hostility to racism and Nazism.

The transfer of loyalty was made easier by the KGB's rigorous suppression of the truth about Soviet society, and by its skilful deception and manipulation of foreign visitors.

The result was an extraordinary suspension of disbelief by large numbers of otherwise intelligent Western observers. The intellectuals were most to blame: by definition, they should have been more resistant to brain-washing than the others. Instead, they broadcast their folly far and wide.

Possibly the most damaging of them were the famous sociologists Sidney and Beatrice Webb. In 1936, impressed, fairly enough, by their monumental *History of Trade Unionism*, I bought a first edition of their massive, meretricious *Soviet Communism: A New Civilization?* which did little more than recycle the propaganda to which they had been exposed on their visit to the Soviet Union. Defiantly, in subsequent editions, the Webbs dropped the question mark from the title.

George Bernard Shaw was another famous Soviet dupe. In 1931, leaving the Soviet Union, he remarked: 'Tomorrow I leave this land of hope and return to our Western countries of despair.' Later Shaw became more critical, and during the war I overheard him at a dinner disparaging Lenin, remarking that of course he, GBS, had read Marx long before Lenin had.

Comparatively few of those who supported the Soviet Union in the early days were genuine proletarians. One, however, was a former boiler-maker, the genial, combative, general secretary of the British Communist Party, Harry Pollitt. I first met him on the Soviet ship on which we were returning from the Soviet Union. By general consent of the passengers, he was allowed to monopolize the single desk space in the ship's small saloon. There he would sit hour after hour writing – it was assumed – a report for his party on the resolutions of the recent Comintern congress. These called for a united front of all progressive forces against fascism and war – a repudiation of the disastrous sectarianism which had led the German communists to fight the German Social Democrats rather than the Nazis and thus open Hitler's road to power.

A War of Words

I felt some admiration for Pollitt, and was inclined to agree with his call for a Western alliance with the Soviet Union in order to contain Nazi Germany. So, when I became president of the Oxford Union, I invited him down to speak. The invitation caused some excitement, and when I was warned that some militant anti-communists were plotting a demonstration against him, I alerted the police. As Pollitt began speaking in the crowded debating chamber, an undergraduate in the gallery drew a bag of flour from underneath his jacket, lobbed it in Pollitt's direction and fled. The bag of flour missed, police whistles sounded everywhere, and the culprit was caught.

Pollitt was the most effective and attractive communist I have known. Even his forlorn, disingenuous defence of Stalin's crimes had a certain dignity:

The thing that mattered to me was that lads like me had whacked the bosses and the landlords, had taken their factories, their lands and their banks ... these are the lads and lassies I must support through thick and thin ... for me these same people could never do, nor ever can do, any wrong against the working class. I wasn't concerned as to whether or not the Russian revolution had caused bloodshed, been violent, and all the rest of it.[1]

Different from Pollitt in every sense, being well-born, eccentric and unreliable, was my Oxford friend, Philip Toynbee. A romantic and wholly misplaced admiration for the Soviet Union's role in the Spanish civil war persuaded him to visit Spain himself and to join the Oxford Communist Party. He must have presented a problem to his fellow members. He was often drunk and pursued women relentlessly, being blacklisted (or so he boasted to me) by a record number of debutantes' mothers.

Toynbee followed me as president of the Oxford Union – the first communist to be elected – and in my speech welcoming him I described him, in Union style, as 'a wild man who needed a nurse, though she, poor girl, would need a chaperone'. Toynbee was a talented writer and after the war was for many years the *Observer*'s leading book reviewer.

But who was a Party member? Who was a fellow-traveller? Who was meretricious *Short History of the Communist Party of the USSR*? Why were communists included among the recipients of letters of thanks I sent to supporters after the 1945 election? (This last point was later used against me in the Commons when I was on the front bench, much to my embarrassment and Attlee's surprise.) And was it my idea, or Jock's, that, as the local Labour candidate, I should march in a demonstration to Carbrooke church, where the vicar, the Revd George Chambers, was an avowed communist, walking behind a crucifix, which was decorated with the hammer and sickle?

Fellow-travellers were less of a problem than 'agents of influence'. When the first archives of the Information Research Department were released by the Foreign Office in August 1995, the IRD and I were attacked with surprising venom in the *Guardian* in a leading article and in the correspondence columns. The author was Richard Gott, who had worked for the *Guardian* for many years, reporting sympathetically on communist causes in Asia and Latin America. In 1977, he was appointed foreign news editor of the *Guardian* and a year later was appointed features editor.

Gott kept his KGB contacts secret, even from his editor, and when these were eventually disclosed (by the KGB defector, Oleg Gordievsky) he did his best to make light of them. For example, he explained: 'The Russians did pay my fare and my hotel to go to Vienna, Athens and Nicosia, to meet their man. So, I have to admit that I took red gold even if only for expenses.'

I have already quoted Gott's attacks on the IRD and myself, which were on familiar Marxist lines. His letter, of 21 August 1995, continued:

A self-proclaimed social democrat and anti-Stalinist, (Lord Mayhew's) only claim to fame was to devise an anti-democratic institution – the Information Research Department of the Foreign Office. ... The tragedy of the activities of Mayhew and his friends was that, in the name of an anti-Stalinism which looked antediluvian by the 1960s, they helped to perpetuate the cold war far beyond its natural span.

The culpability of Soviet sympathizers is to be measured partly by

loyal to the Party but told not to become a member? Having decli
MI5's invitation to join them, I found it almost impossible to
When I suggested to Attlee in 1947 that the Whip should be remo
from half a dozen Labour MPs, I had no idea to which category t
belonged. (Attlee himself would have known, however, as MI5
fully penetrated the Communist Party at that time.)

Much the ablest and most influential of the fellow-travellers
D. N. ('Johnny') Pritt KC, a successful barrister and chairman
various communist front organizations. Pritt disliked me, and on
occasion complained to my superior, the Minister of State, that
official letters to him were discourteous. He may have had s(
justification for this, and Hector McNeil sent me a mild rebuke.

Pritt was an expert defender of the indefensible. About the So
penal system he wrote:

*The Russians apply fully and logically the theory that imprisonment n
be reformatory and not in the smallest degree punitive, and they reg
society as sharing with the criminal the responsibility of his crime ... (
succeed in creating in their penal establishments a very stril
atmosphere of cooperative endeavour to effect a real cure of bad ha
and a full restoration to the normal life of society and to the right.
citizenship.*[2]

Among the half-dozen fellow-travelling MPs expelled from the P;
was another able barrister, John Platts-Mills, MP for Finsbury. After
had been deselected and replaced by a new Labour candidate, I
asked to go to a public meeting in Finsbury town hall to support
new candidate and explain the government's foreign policy. It was
rowdiest meeting I have ever addressed.

Must I also classify as a fellow-traveller my old agent in sor
Norfolk, Jock Watson? He was a good-natured, lionhearted, cli
footed Clydesider. Before the war, we canvassed the villages of sor
Norfolk in friendship and complete harmony. Only now, looki
back, do I have my doubts. Why was I not warned about the in
tration of communists into the South Norfolk Labour Party wher
was away at the war? Why was Jock so enthusiastic about Stali

the date when they were duped. In the 1920s and 1930s the Soviet Union was remote and mysterious, and Stalinist illusions could be more easily understood. But for those who maintained contact with the KGB into the 1990s, one could argue that they showed a breathtaking lack of judgement and integrity.

And where did Felix Greene stand in these matters? In 1957, I had arranged with BBC TV to make two documentaries to mark the fortieth anniversary of the October Revolution, and travelled to the Soviet Union and China to seek permission for a BBC camera team to enter these countries and do some filming. In both countries I received the same reply: visas would not be granted for the BBC cameramen, but the governments would be pleased to cooperate with me in producing a joint film 'for the purpose of increasing friendship and understanding between the peoples'. I would be provided with film teams, studios, travel facilities – even an orchestra. The final version of the film would be approved by both sides. In reply to my questions, it was explained that the inclusion of negative material, for instance about human rights or housing shortages, would not be consistent with the purpose of the film.

It was clear that these proposed films – lavish, colourful, friendly, and showing aspects of Soviet and Chinese life still quite unknown in the West – would be immensely popular and successful. At the same time they would misrepresent the Chinese and Soviet social system and mislead Western viewers. So, with the BBC's full support, I turned these offers down. Not so ITV, with a keener eye on its ratings. It agreed to show two films directed by complacent Western commentators and approved by the Soviet and Chinese governments. When broadcast, they made a strong and favourable impact on millions of undiscriminating Western viewers.

This was a new form of communist censorship – by choice of a Western commentator. The Chinese government chose Felix Greene, a strongly Sinophile film maker. A French journalist, Jacques Marcuse, who was in China with Greene, and watched him at work, took him to task for being manipulated by Chinese stage managers. He wrote 'After that, I saw no more of him, except from a distance when, for instance, he was filming Wang Fu Ching [the avenue], which had been cleared of traffic and down which a sprinkler was operating – a thing never witnessed before in broad daylight.'[3]

A TV commentator who shared my concern at this debasement of our profession was my friend Aidan Crawley, a former MP and minister, and subsequently a director of ITN. He agreed to come with me to make a protest to Charles Hill, who was then ITV's chairman. Hill arranged for us to see Greene's film again, together with himself and his director, Sir Robert Fraser. Scarcely had the film started, with some shots of traffic in Peking, than Crawley and I uttered cries of derision. Hill stopped the film: what on earth could be wrong with that? 'What about the cars?' we asked. 'Where had they come from? Where were the bicycles and rickshaws?' Hill and Fraser were impressed, and the film show was quickly abandoned. Whether our protest had any impact on ITV's subsequent programming of communist issues, I do not know.

In fact, however, my visit to China had not been entirely unsuccessful. I became friendly with David Chipp, Reuters' highly intelligent and resourceful correspondent in China, who was then the only Western journalist in the entire country. He had a small tourist cine camera, and gallantly agreed to travel around the countryside with me, filming a collective farm and other aspects of country life in China. At some personal risk, I smuggled this film through customs at Peking airport, and included it in my programme on Chinese communism. Though of poor quality, it was, I believe, the first freely shot film of China to be shown on Western television.

The largest and politically the most important category of the Soviet Union's 'foreign friends' were what Lenin called 'useful idiots'. For six months in the 1930s, as I have already confessed, I was a 'useful idiot' myself. I visited the Soviet Union in 1935 and afterwards spread idiotically favourable views of communist achievements. George Orwell once wrote memorably: 'One sometimes got the impression that the mere words "Socialism" and "Communism" draw towards them with magnetic force every fruit juice drinker, nudist, sandal-wearer, sex-maniac, Quaker, "Nature Cure" quack, pacifist and feminist in England.'[4] However, this is, in my view, to omit the most important group. If he had been writing after the war, I think Orwell would certainly have included in his catalogue many unilateralists and representatives of the Labour left. These were the well-meaning people who, without being communists, urged that Stalin should be given the secrets of the atom bomb; that British troops should be withdrawn from Greece; that the rearmament of Germany was a crime and would provoke world war; that Alger Hiss was innocent; that Polaris should be scrapped. Without being communists, they viewed politics as a struggle of the working class against the capitalist class. They were members of a 'working-class movement', regularly referring to the working class as 'our people'.

A good example was the left-wing Labour MP, Konni Zilliacus. A large, shambling, amiable person, who had served in the League of Nations secretariat between the wars, he was a good linguist and very knowledgeable about foreign affairs. He was never a communist, and it was accurately stated by Ian Mikardo MP – who was in a very good position to know – that 'Zilliacus forms his views quite independently of the communists or anyone else and holds them with complete and selfless sincerity.'[5]

In innumerable prolix speeches and newspaper articles, Zilliacus blamed the East–West confrontation entirely on the irrational hostility of the West towards the East. Typically, he took me to task, in a long letter in the *Manchester Guardian* (10 May 1946) over the critically important decision of the German Social Democrats not to merge with the German communists.

If the Labour Party leadership had done nothing to oppose unity of action between socialists and communists, I do not believe that any of us 27 MPs would have felt it necessary to send a message to the German Social Democratic Congress in Berlin testifying to our support for cooperation and unity between socialists and communists on terms fair to both. We did so in order to counteract the wholly unauthorized action of one Labour MP, Mr Christopher Mayhew, and some of the leaders of the Labour Party in conveying the impression to the German workers that the Labour policy was one of hostility to unity of action between socialists and communists in Germany.

We did so because the present anti-unity campaign on the continent of the Labour Party's leaders and of the Labour Government is not only unauthorized by the Party as a whole but in flat contradiction to the whole tenor of discussions on this subject at successive annual conferences of the Labour Party.

In 1949, after speaking at a communist-controlled peace rally in Paris, contrary to Labour Party rules, Zilliacus – still an independent minded non-communist – was expelled from the Party. He had been useful to the communist cause in a well-meant but idiotic manner.

The same can be said of a very different and much more important left-wing Labour MP. I remember standing next to Tony Benn while we sang the Red Flag at the end of a Party conference. After singing, with some misgivings, that the red flag 'has shrouded oft our martyred dead', I turned to him. 'Name three martyrs, Tony.' After a pause, the reply came 'The Peterloo massacre'. This was a brave effort but confirmed that if the red flag had ever shrouded a British corpse, at least it had not done so for over 130 years.

Benn was – is – personable, articulate, industrious, intelligent and – usually – good-tempered. Like Zilliacus he was never a communist and formed his views independently of communists. Yet his quasi-Marxist views often led him into activities useful to the communist cause.

His diary (1973–6) shows plainly his sympathy for Marxists and communists and his willingness to accept them as allies.

1 May 1973

It was a beautiful day and we marched for two or three miles with 25,000 people. . . . Outside the town hall all the sects were selling their papers: the International Marxists Red Weekly; *the Socialist Labour League with* Workers Press; *the International Socialists with* The Socialist Worker; *the Communist Party with* The Morning Star; *the Labour Party with* Labour Weekly. *This getting around the labour movement of all these sects was a very important part of the exercise, and we bought all the papers. . . . Dick Etheridge, who is a communist, spoke and he made the collection speech brilliantly. He was tremendously informal and friendly.*[6]

Benn was a highly influential Party leader throughout the 1970s, and in 1973 he was able to persuade the National Executive Committee to abandon the 'proscribed list', which prevented Labour Party members from joining communist front organizations. The result was a further influx of Marxists and fellow-travellers into the Party.

I was by now despairing of the Labour Party. 'Old Labour' was opening the door to the enemies of democracy.

The last straw, for me, was the domination by Marxists of a committee set up to frame a policy for the Party on the media.[7] Tony Benn was the chairman. Eventually, I wrote to him in exasperation:

As you know, I have been worried by your handling as Chairman of the Communications Advisory Committee, and feel I should put the reasons on paper: (1) I do not understand why our two main recommendations – both extremely left-wing – were only put before us at our sixth and supposedly final meeting. Could you tell me who put these proposals into our draft report, and why he did not bring them forward earlier? (2) I'm not clear who selected the members of the committee and on what basis. They seem to be quite unrepresentative of Party opinion . . . (3) A smaller point. I was surprised that, without previous discussion, you provided slips of paper at our last meeting for us to sign to commit ourselves to the report. This struck me as unusual and questionable, especially since no slips were provided for those of us who disagreed with the report.

These are all procedural objections, but I must also record my strong belief that the committee's principal recommendation ('the controlling body of each broadcasting production unit should be elected by the workers engaged in the enterprise, based on the trade union structure') constitutes, in view of the political orientation of the main trade union concerned, a serious threat to democratic freedom. As you will know, six of the eight officers of the ACCT (Association of Cinematograph, Television and Allied Technicians) are either communists or Trotskyists, and the General Secretary has long supported organizations which are pro-communist and were until recently proscribed by our Party. Fortunately, there is a growing rank and file movement in the ACCT to get these people out, but in the meantime our proposals would give them considerable potential for censorship and programme control.

I would be grateful for some reassurance from you on these points.

I am sending copies of this, in the first instance, to our Party colleagues on the working party, and to the Chairman of the Home Policy Committee.

Benn replied politely, but his diary (of 28 January 1974) gives his version of this meeting.

We went through the communications Green Paper and the main argument was whether an element of industrial democracy should be included. Chris Mayhew argued strongly that the mass media were too important to let democracy be applied, he was pretty much in a minority. There was a division at seven and I walked out with Chris Mayhew who said 'this is disgusting, woolly, Marxist stuff. You'll have communists running newspapers.' 'What about William Rees-Mogg?' I said, and I recited what had happened in The Times: 'I'd rather have William Rees-Mogg running newspapers, given he believes in parliamentary democracy, than Alan Sapper and the Marxists.' I said 'that's just an indication that you feel socially more at ease with William Rees-Mogg than you do with a prominent trade union leader.' He was angry. It is not really worth having him on the committee but I have to take account of his view.[8]

Fortunately, there were still at that time enough responsible people left in the Labour Party. They did take my view into account, and Benn's recommendation was stillborn. But as late as 1984 he was still unconcerned about communist influence in the media, declaring on one occasion 'The *Morning Star* is overwhelmingly the best newspaper in Britain.'[9] If Lenin had been alive in those years, and had been asked to nominate Britain's most characteristic 'useful idiot', he would most surely have chosen Tony Benn.

Chapter 6
Cold War: Reflections, Doubts and Some Regrets

It was mid-winter 1984, my seventh visit to the Soviet Union. This time I went as the defence spokesman of the Liberal Party, accompanying our party leader, Sir David Steel and our foreign affairs spokesman, Sir Russell Johnson. We flew to Moscow on a private plane, laid on by a wealthy colleague and fellow passenger, Sir Anthony Jacobs. There had just been a heavy fall of snow, and when I looked down as we came in to land, I could see no sign of life at all, just a vast blanket of snow. This impression of Soviet lifelessness stayed with me throughout the visit. Everything and everyone seemed lifeless – the people in the streets, the half-empty hotels, the huge, ugly new buildings. At that time, the Soviet economy was registering zero growth. The Soviet leader, Yuri Andropov, was terminally ill, and was to die a few days after we returned to the United Kingdom.

Our meetings with high Soviet officials were also lifeless. They would read out, from carefully prepared texts, the Soviet position on various aspects of nuclear disarmament, and we would then follow with predictable suggestions and questions, to which we would receive predictable replies.

Nevertheless, this was a time of acute tension in East–West relations. President Ronald Reagan was striving, openly and successfully, to establish military and economic domination over the Soviet Union, predicting with clumsy rhetoric the inevitable dissolution of the 'evil empire'. In response, Andropov had launched a panic measure, an extraordinary operation named 'Ryan' (Raketno-Yadernoye Napadenie). This instructed the KGB and Soviet embassies overseas to report in detail not *whether* the United States was preparing a nuclear first strike, of which Andropov had no doubt, but *when* they were intending to launch it. In scores of countries, Soviet diplomats and KGB officials, fearful for their careers, were feeding these delusions with supportive 'evidence', which in many cases they themselves disbelieved. Even Oleg Gordievsky, who was then working secretly for MI6 while head of the KGB in London, has confessed to taking part in this dangerous charade. Some years later, he admitted to me that he was genuinely afraid at the time that Andropov, in a Ryan-induced panic, might decide to 'get his retaliation in first'.[1]

I urged David Steel to loosen our meetings up, but this was not his style. At one meeting, a senior Soviet official, anxious to demonstrate the aggressive intentions of the capitalist world, made the familiar, dreary point that Winston Churchill had once advocated 'strangling Bolshevism at birth'. So he had, of course; and the Soviet people might have suffered less if he had succeeded. But my eye was caught by a portrait of Lenin behind this official's chair. Lenin's whole life had been devoted to strangling capitalism. Why not point this out? Why not ask the official what contribution his revered role model had made to peace and friendship between the socialist and capitalist worlds?

There was a time when I would have done this willingly; but now I was a junior member of a goodwill delegation, and was also, I have to admit, beginning to feel my age. After nearly fifty years, arguments about Lenin had lost their novelty. Moreover, for some years past my views on the cold war had been changing. After the Soviet invasion of Czechoslovakia in 1968, the world communist movement, which had been losing momentum for many years, virtually disintegrated. In one country after another, pro-Soviet communist parties drifted rightwards or split or simply subsided. Where it survived, Marxism became the creed of the Trotskyites, bitterly hostile to the Soviet Union. Thus, throughout the 1970s, I came increasingly to doubt whether the Soviet Union any longer presented an ideological, economic or political threat to the West.

Indeed, the boot was now on the other foot. It was now the West that was presenting the challenge to the East, demanding democratic rights for dissidents in the communist world, and other reforms laid down in the Helsinki Agreements, which presented threats to the

Cold War: Reflections, Doubts and Some Regrets

integrity of communist regimes. (At the Liberal delegation's meetings with Ambassador Sir Iain Sutherland in Moscow, this was the sole subject of our discussion.)

At the same time, Reagan was setting a pace in an economic and military build up which the Soviet Union was incapable of matching, and was also provocatively forecasting the collapse of the Soviet system.

Andropov's operation 'Ryan', assuming a nuclear first strike by the United States, was the irrational product of a paranoid imagination, but for that very reason raised the nightmare possibility of a pre-emptive Soviet nuclear strike.

For these reasons, in the mid-1970s I began suggesting that the Western powers should open discussions with the Soviet Union on the possibility of a European settlement – phased, mutual disengagement of NATO and the Warsaw Pact forces from central Europe, combined with German reunification.

This was in fact very similar to a proposal made by Bulganin in 1957 – who no doubt believed, foolishly, that the unified Germany would be communist – and would probably have been acceptable to any Soviet government in the 1970s and 1980s. During our 1984 Moscow visit, when I put the ideas forward privately to various officials, they responded very positively. However, the proposals were unacceptable to my Liberal colleagues and positively anathema in the West. I put them forward at one of the famous Königswinter conferences, attended by leading British and German politicians and media pundits. I found the conference not merely opposed to the ideas, but outraged by them. The two Germanys were felt to have drifted so far apart that it was both impracticable and undesirable to reunite them. In addition, reunification would fatally disrupt NATO. Particular distaste was shown for a statement I made that the division of Germany was 'unnatural'. The distinguished historian, Sir Michael Howard, commented amid applause that if I thought that German unity was the natural state of Germany, it showed a remarkable ignorance of German history. I was prevented from raising the topic again at the conference, and though hitherto a regular attender, was never again invited to Königswinter.

Nor did my ideas fare much better when I aired them at the North Atlantic Assembly of which I was a member, nor when I wrote them in the correspondence columns of *The Times*, the *Guardian* and the *Independent*. The best I could manage was to get a friendly resolution through the Liberal Assembly at Bournemouth in 1984 – though even then the hated phrase 'German reunification' had to be omitted: 'Concerned at the growing conflict between the demand for self-determination in Germany and eastern Europe and the Soviet Union's perception of its security interests, Assembly believes that initiatives should be investigated for overcoming this problem including the mutual and balanced disengagement of Soviet and American forces.'

I would have liked to have raised these ideas during our delegation meetings in Moscow. At least, they would have led to livelier discussions. Instead, for myself, the most memorable feature of our visit was a guided tour of Lenin's modest office and bedroom in the Kremlin. These had been preserved as Lenin left them. Here were the pens, the spectacles, the pamphlets, speeches and books that had launched the Russian revolution, and that, Lenin believed, would spread it into the heart of Europe. Here were copies of his aptly named newspaper *Iskra* (the Spark), which was to light the fuse.

I could imagine Lenin sitting at this desk (perhaps using one of the pens being pointed out in reverent tones by our guide), and writing such orders as these: 'We have to encourage energetic and massive terror'; 'The plan for a mass collection of grain using machine guns is a brilliant one.' 'Shoot the conspirators and waverers without asking anyone'; 'Draw up district lists of the wealthiest peasants who will answer with their lives for all grain surpluses.'[2]

Lenin marked some of his letters 'Not for copying'. These included an order that resulted in the killing of 14,200 priests. Another authorized payments of huge subsidies to foreign communist parties (including 200,000 gold roubles to the British Communist Party) – this at a time when millions of Soviet peasant families were starving to death.[3]

The release of Soviet archives now shows clearly that it was Lenin, not Stalin, who began the series of barbaric atrocities against the Soviet people. Lenin was not only a cruel and ruthless fanatic, but his monomaniacal obsession with class drew him consistently into wrong political judgements. Obsessed by the conviction that class – not nationality, religion, culture or ethnicity – was the determinant of historical change, his predictions of developments at home and abroad were often childishly mistaken.

Yet, at the last count, 653 million copies of this man's books had been published worldwide. In his study in the Kremlin, I recalled that one of them, *Imperialism* (or was it *State and Revolution?*), had figured in my recommended reading list at Oxford, and that I had been influenced by it, and had then reacted against it. This seemed to vindicate the free circulation of bad ideas; but it also made me feel resentful on my own account. How had I allowed this cruel, arrogant and misguided fanatic to play such a large part in my life? But for Lenin there would have been no cold war, and but for the cold war my political career would certainly have been much more constructive and enjoyable. Thanks to Lenin, confrontation with Marxists has always been unusually venomous. Lenin set the fashion of Marxist vituperation: his opponents were never simply misguided, they were 'traitors', 'vermin', 'swine'.

A famous international socialist, Karl Kautsky, was a 'renegade', 'swindler', 'sycophant of the bourgeoisie', 'yesman of scoundrels and bloodsuckers', 'only fit for the cesspit of renegades'.[4] Stalin followed suit, and a tradition was established among Marxists of denouncing their opponents in the most venomous terms. Even at the lowest level, opponents of Marxism such as myself were regularly denounced as 'splitters', 'traitors', 'careerists' and so on.

Today, in academic circles, especially in the United States, the view that the cold war started with Lenin is unfashionable.

We are taught that the cold war was essentially a power struggle between the Soviet Union and the United States which began in 1947 when the two powers fell out over the future of Germany and eastern Europe. This view is well illustrated by the recently published American book *We All Lost the Cold War* by Ned Lebow and Janice Stein. Thus, the massive index to this book contains some 400 references to President Kennedy and no references at all to Ernest Bevin or Clement Attlee. Lenin wins two references but no other

Europeans are referred to except Harold Macmillan (twice) and Konrad Adenauer (once). The Comintern and Cominform are not listed. Like other books and learned articles published across the Atlantic, the Lebow–Stein book downplays the ideological war – the challenge of Marxism-Leninism, and the West's response to it – as well as the contributions to the cold war of the United Kingdom and other participants besides the United States. It necessarily deals with the postwar communism of Spain, Germany, Hungary, Greece and Czechoslovakia.[5]

A common-sense definition of the cold war would be the struggle for power between the communist and capitalist worlds by all means short of armed conflict between them. This definition would exclude the armed conflict of the wars of intervention after the First World War, and also, of course, the Second World War. But it would rightly include Lenin's founding of the Comintern. This aggressive move can be looked upon fairly as a declaration of cold war against the capitalist world. The challenge was made by Lenin and the West's response followed. This response had a moral purpose – the defence of democracy against Marxism. As relations between the Soviet Union and the United States degenerated into a nihilistic struggle for power, the moral purpose of the West's resistance to Soviet communism became undermined. Thus, the West can be blamed for prolonging the cold war needlessly. During the 1980s, Reagan's strategy of forcing expenditure on the Soviet Union, his race to nuclear superiority, his plans for a Strategic Defence Initiative, his acceptance of nuclear weapons as war-fighting materials, and the propagation of the myth of a Soviet lead in nuclear armament produced operation 'Ryan', and increased the chance of nuclear catastrophe.

Notes

Chapter 1

1. Exceptionally able and intelligent, David Nenk became a high-flyer in the civil service but died tragically young, from cancer.
2. Christopher Mayhew, *Time to Explain: An Autobiography* (Century Hutchinson, London, 1987) Chapter 2.
3. *University Forward*, May 1937.

Chapter 2

1. Appendix 1, Extracts of memorandum, C. Mayhew to E. Bevin, urging establishment of the IRD.
2. Appendix 2, Cabinet Paper (48) 8, 4 January 1948. *Future Foreign Publicity Policy*, PRO CAB 129/23.
3. Anatole Goldberg, interview with Lyn Smith, 1980.
4. Dr George Urban, in conversation with C. Mayhew, 13 November 1996.
5. Hugh Greene, interview with Lyn Smith, 1980.
6. Appendix 3, Extracts from Foreign Office Circular 0121, 17 August 1948, *Directive for Propaganda Countering Soviet Attacks on 'Colonialism' and Colonial Administrations*.
7. Appendix 4, Extracts from C. Mayhew's speeches to Committee 3 of the UN General Assembly, 4 and 15 October 1948.
8. However, at the UN in October/November 1947, Grantley Adams had himself deflated Soviet attacks on British colonial oppression by pointing out that the legislature in Barbados had been independent for several hundred years.
9. Appendix 5, Letter C. Mayhew to Mr A. A. Arutiunian, 31 October 1947.
10. Letter, Tony Harrison to C. Mayhew, 25 August 1995.
11. Sir Hugh Greene, interview with Lyn Smith, 1980.

Chapter 3

1. Letter, Sir Ian Jacob to C. Mayhew, 12 November 1954.
2. Memo to Charles Hill, 9 December 1957.

3. Memo, C. Mayhew to Foreign Office, 28 October 1958.
4. S. Volkov, *Testimony: The Memoirs of Shostakovich* (Hamish Hamilton, London, 1979) p. 151.
5. Tom Bower, *Robert Maxwell: The Final Verdict* (Harper Collins, New York, 1996) pp. 156–7.
6. Letter, C. Mayhew to Barnett Janner MP, 28 July 1959.

Chapter 4

1. A. Howard, *Crossman: The Pursuit of Power* (Jonathan Cape, London, 1990) p. 233.
2. N. Lebow and J. Stein, *We All Lost the Cold War* (Princeton University Press, New Jersey, 1994) Chapter 7.
3. Mayhew, *Time to Explain*, op. cit., Chapter 17.
4. Letter, Lord Mayhew to David Steel, 12 March 1982.
5. Hetty Vorhaus, letter to the *Guardian*.
6. Letter, Edward Lucas, freelance journalist, 17 September 1989.

Chapter 5

1. Kevin Morgan, *Harry Pollitt* (Manchester University Press, Manchester, 1993) p. 177.
2. P. Hollander, *Political Pilgrims: Travels of Western Intellectuals to the Soviet Union, China and Cuba 1928–78* (Oxford University Press, Oxford, 1981) pp. 143–4.
3. Jacques Marcuse, *Peking Papers*, pp. 106–7, cited in Hollander, *Political Pilgrims*, op. cit., p. 399.
4. George Orwell, *The Road to Wigan Pier* (Victor Gollancz, London, 1937) p. 152.
5. *Tribune*, 4 March 1949, quoted in M. Jones, *Michael Foot* (Victor Gollancz, London, 1994) p. 153.
6. Tony Benn, *Against the Tide: Diaries 1973–76* (Century Hutchinson, London, 1989) p. 23.
7. C. Mayhew, *Time to Explain*, op. cit., p. 203.
8. Tony Benn, *Against the Tide*, op. cit., p. 98.
9. *Morning Star*, 6 October 1984.

Chapter 6

1. Oleg Gordievsky, in conversation with Lord Mayhew, 1996.

Notes

2. Dimitri Volkogonov, *Lenin: Life and Legacy* (Harper Collins, New York, 1994) p. 271.
3. Volkogonov, *Lenin*, op. cit., p. 399.
4. Volkogonov, *Lenin*, op. cit., p. 179.
5. Lebow and Stern, *We All Lost the Cold War*, op. cit.

Appendix 1
Extracts of Memorandum, C. Mayhew to E. Bevin, urging establishment of IRD

They arrived at Lake Success this year with huge briefs for defensive and offensive propaganda purposes, and with no intention whatever for making an effort towards international cooperation. Their long and carefully prepared speeches, frequently irrelevant to the agenda, were plainly addressed to a wider audience than the assembly – to their own people at home and to communists, fellow-travellers and doubters abroad. Though badly received by the great majority of delegates, these speeches undoubtedly had propaganda value. The Slavs clearly regard the United Nations as a useful instrument of political warfare. There was in practice no effective cooperation between East and West through United Nations machinery. Through such links as remain, it can easily be argued that the UN hampers rather than encourages international cooperation. Moreover, if the United Nations did not exist, or the Slavs were outside it, the way would be clearer for closer cooperation between the countries of Western Europe – or at least between the great majority of these countries. Fear of 'by-passing the United Nations' still exercises a restraining influence on many of these countries, and communist delegates seize every opportunity of playing on these fears and of putting themselves in the position of defending the United Nations against the disloyalty of some of its members...

It might perhaps be argued that at least the discussions and personal contacts at the UN have a salutary effect on the communist delegates themselves. But in conversations with the communists it was impossible to detect any seeds of doubt sown by the speeches of other delegates. This might have been the fault of these speeches, but was

Extracts of Memorandum, C. Mayhew to E. Bevin

also easily accounted for by the delegates' thorough indoctrination, their natural loyalty to their home country, by fear and self-interest and by the plausibility of their Marxist analysis. However, I would dismiss suggestions being aired by United States delegates, that the Soviet Union should be expelled from the United Nations. Any such initiative would violate what should be the cardinal principle of our foreign policy – viz., that we take no step in the direction of dividing East and West unless (a) it is obviously forced on us by the East, (b) it is obviously impracticable to do otherwise, e.g. Germany, (c) it is impossible to resist the demands of public opinion in our own country. If we do not strictly adhere to this principle we leave our left flank open, in the long years ahead, to the false but dangerous accusation of having repelled the Soviet Union while she was still willing to cooperate. This factor is so important, in my view, as to be completely overriding. . . .

To sum up, I think that we should not in any way attempt to manoeuvre the Slav bloc out of the UN, and should discourage possible future attempts by [the] USA to do this; but that we should not sacrifice any chance of greater integration of Western Europe through inhibitions about 'by-passing [the] UN', and that we should go to future UN meetings well prepared for a propaganda counter-offensive. . . . I feel that after November, if the Council of Foreign Ministers fails, we should launch a sustained, offensive propaganda campaign, aimed at countering the Cominform and weakening communist pressure generally and in particular in France, Germany, Italy, Greece and the Middle East.

Our campaign should be based on the following principles:

1. It should be as positive as possible. We should sell social democracy as strongly as we attempt to discredit communism. The fact that social democratic goods are temporarily somewhat shop-soiled is no reason for holding back. We must make the best of the goods we have got. Where necessary we should admit our difficulties and show how they can be and are being overcome by democratic methods. We must avoid at all costs appearing to oppose communism as defenders of the status quo. Our propaganda should

Appendix 1

have a challenging 'left' slant and should freely attack the evils of the past, including the failures and injustices of prewar capitalism.

2. We should stress the weakness of communism, not its strength. Contemporary American propaganda is worse than useless. Besides being entirely negative it lays continual stress on the strength and aggressiveness of communism. This increases the fears, and unbalances the judgement of those who are already anti-communist, and raises the confidence of Western communists and fellow-travellers, for whom the strength of communism is itself a proof of their theories. ... Far more effective would be a propaganda campaign which showed – far more truthfully – that Russia is for the most part a poor, backward, devastated country, with the ridiculous pretension to be 'the workers' paradise' and 'the champion of the oppressed.'

3. In order to justify propaganda activities in foreign countries, our campaign would take the form of a defence of Britain, the British Commonwealth and Empire, and British social democracy against communist propaganda attack. But in effect it would be a positive attack on the weak points of communist theory and practice. ... It would draw comparisons with Russian standards of living, workers' houses, social services, citizens' rights, free press, etc. Subject to high-level 'vetting', it could be used to expound and defend the Marshall Plan and other foreign policy issues over which we are at odds with the communists, and it could contrast the attitude at [the] UN of the democratic and the communist powers. It would be truthful, well documented and closely argued, and should be designed for journalists, public speakers, trade unionists, and political organisers etc. at home and abroad who are up against communist opposition. ...

Appendix 2
Memorandum by the Secretary of State for Foreign Affairs

THIS DOCUMENT IS THE PROPERTY OF HIS BRITANNIC MAJESTY'S GOVERNMENT

Printed for the Cabinet. January 1948

TOP SECRET PRO CAB 129/23 Copy No. 43
C.P. (48) 8
4th January, 1948

CABINET

FUTURE FOREIGN PUBLICITY POLICY

MEMORANDUM BY THE SECRETARY OF STATE FOR FOREIGN AFFAIRS

In my paper on "The First Aim of British Foreign Policy" (C.P. (48) 6) I have shown that the Russian and the Communist Allies are threatening the whole fabric of Western civilisation, and I have drawn attention to the need to mobilise spiritual forces, as well as material and political, for its defence. It is for us, as Europeans and as a Social Democratic Government, and not the Americans, to give the lead in the spiritual, moral and political sphere to all the democratic elements in Western Europe which are anti-Communist and, at the same time, genuinely progressive and reformist, believing in freedom, planning and social justice – what one might call the "Third Force." Equally in the Middle East and possibly in certain Far Eastern countries such as India, Burma, Ceylon, Malaya, Indonesia and Indo-China, Commu-

Appendix 2

nism will make headway unless a strong spiritual and moral lead on the above lines is given against it, and we are in a good position to give such a lead. In many countries of Western Europe the forces of Social Democracy will be the mainstay, but even in Western Europe and obviously in the Middle East and Far East our appeal could not be only to Social Democratic Parties.

Soviet propaganda has, since the end of the war, carried on in every sphere a vicious attack against the British Commonwealth and against Western democracy. Our publicity has hitherto been confined to supporting and explaining the current policy of His Majesty's Government in foreign affairs and at home, to advocating our way of life, and publicising our social-democratic programme and achievements. Except in the Middle East, where we have allowed ourselves more latitude our propaganda where Russia and Communism are concerned, has been non-provocative, and we have not attempted systematically to expose the myths of the Soviet paradise. Something far more positive is clearly now required. If we are to give a moral lead to the forces of anti-Communism in Europe and Asia, we must be prepared to pass over to the offensive and not leave the initiative to the enemy, but make them defend themselves.

Recommendations

1. We should adopt a new line in our foreign publicity designed to oppose the inroads of Communism, by taking the offensive against it, basing ourselves on the standpoint of the position and vital ideas of British Social Democracy and Western civilisation, and to give a lead to our friends abroad and help them in the anti-Communist struggle.

2. The only new machinery required would be a small Section in the Foreign Office to collect information concerning Communist policy, tactics and propaganda and to provide material for our anti-Communist publicity through our Missions and Information Services abroad. The fullest co-operation of the BBC Overseas Services would be desirable; but this and the provision of the necessary material by the Central Office of Information would be arranged through the usual channels.

Our anti-Communist publicity material should also be available to

Memorandum by the Secretary of State for Foreign Affairs

Ministers for use, when convenient, in their public speeches; and also to British delegations to conferences and – on an informal basis – to Labour Party and Trades Union delegations.

3. We should develop visits by important Trade Unionists from abroad and other influential, non-Communist foreigners, and set up a "Wilton Park" in which we could offer them courses on British life and institutions, and make available to them material and ideas useful for the struggle in their own countries against Communism. In short, we should seek to make London the Mecca for Social Democrats in Europe.

Considerations

Soviet propaganda has, since the end of the war, been directly hostile to this country, and for many months past has reverted to its old pre-war line of direct antagonism to Social Democracy. As my colleagues are aware, the Prime Minister and I, and other members of the Government, are often directly attacked. The propaganda of the Soviet satellites now, of course, follows exactly the same line, and is apparently to be co-ordinated by the Cominform. We can no longer submit passively to the Communist offensive; we must attack and expose Communism and offer something far better. What we have to offer in contrast to totalitarian Communism and *laissez-faire* capitalism are the vital and progressive ideas of British Social Democracy and Western European civilisation.

I suggest that the following are the principles which should guide our publicity: –

(a) We should advertise our principles as offering the best and most efficient way of life. We should attack, by comparison, the principles and practice of Communism, and also the inefficiency, social injustice and moral weakness of unrestrained capitalism. We must not, however, attack or appear to be attacking any member of the Commonwealth or the United States.

(b) Our main target should be the broad masses of workers and peasants in Europe and the Middle East. We should, therefore, use the arguments most likely to appeal to them. First amongst these is the argument that, compared with Social Democratic countries,

Appendix 2

such as Britain, Sweden and New Zealand, the standard of life (wages, food, housing, &c.) for the ordinary people is extremely low in the Soviet Union, where "privilege for the few" is a growing phenomenon. Russia's pretence to be a "Workers' Paradise" is a gigantic hoax. We can fairly ask why the Communists, if life under Communist rule is so enviable, should shut themselves off so completely. Social Democracy, on the other hand, gives higher living standards for the masses and protects them against privilege and exploitation, whether Capitalist or Communist.

(c) Equally important is that we should stress the civil liberties issues, pointing to the many analogies between Hitlerite and Communist systems. We cannot hope successfully to repel Communism only by disparaging it on material grounds, and must add a positive appeal to Democratic and Christian principles, remembering the strength of Christian sentiment in Europe. We must put forward a positive rival ideology. We must stand on the broad principles of Social Democracy, which, in fact, has its basis in the value of civil liberty and human rights. Examples should be given in order to show what the loss of civil liberties and human rights means in practice. This is specially necessary in countries where the loss of these rights and liberties has never been experienced and therefore is not appreciated.

(d) We should represent Communism and the foreign policy of Communist countries as a hindrance to international co-operation and world peace. We should expose the immorality, militancy and destructiveness of Communist foreign policy, and diplomatic methods, their manoeuvres to divide and impoverish Western European countries and to exploit their control of Europe's main food-producing areas. We should represent the satellite countries as "Russia's new colonial empire," serving Russia's strategic and economic interests at the cost of the freedom and living standards of the Eastern European peoples. The myth that the Russians never break treaties should be exposed, and Communism portrayed as the stalking-horse of Russian imperialism.

(e) Finally we should disseminate clear and cogent answers to Russian misrepresentations about Britain. We should not make the mistake

Memorandum by the Secretary of State for Foreign Affairs

of allowing ourselves to be drawn into concentrating our whole energy in dealing with those subjects which are selected for debate by Russian propaganda. On the other hand we must see to it that our friends in Europe and elsewhere are armed with the facts and the answers to Russian propaganda. If we do not provide this ammunition, they will not get it from any other source.

In general we should emphasise the weakness of Communism rather than its strength. Contemporary American propaganda, which stresses the strength and aggressiveness of Communism, tends to scare and unbalance the anti-Communists, while heartening the fellow-travellers and encouraging the Communists to bluff more extravagantly. Our propaganda, by dwelling on Russian's [sic] poverty and backwardness, could be expected to relax rather than to raise the international tension.

We must not, of course, exaggerate the effects which can be produced by publicity alone. But I am convinced that in the interests of this country, the British Commonwealth and of our friends abroad, we must now take this more definitely anti-Communist line in our publicity. I ask for the active support and co-operation of my colleagues.

E.B.

Foreign Office, S.W.1,
4th January, 1948

Appendix 3
Extracts from Circular 0121, Foreign Office, 17 August 1948

Directive for Propaganda countering Soviet attacks on 'Colonialism' and Colonial Administrations.

(2) For the world in general, our main line of counterattack on this type of propaganda should be to expose the exploitation and enslavement of weaker countries by Soviet imperialism – e.g. the Baltic States, Iron Curtain countries, Yugoslavia and Manchuria. It is preferable to attack Russian colonial exploitation of countries beyond her borders than to attack discrimination by the more advanced areas of the Soviet Union against backward territories of the union such as the central Asian Republics. But it is essential that we should present against the contrast of the progress of peoples under British aegis from backward status to independence, the regression from independence to oppression and indeed in some cases to annihilation which characterises the Soviet system.

(3) Closely related to this publicity must be that on forced labour, which is a vast subject in itself. It would be wrong, however, to assume that the 'backward' peoples of the Soviet Union have been special victims of forced labour. The mass of evidence available points to a policy of press-gang recruitment by the Secret Police, on the slightest of evidence, on suspicion, or on no discernible grounds at all, impartially applied to Russia proper as to the other republics – though the Ukrainians and other basically dissatisfied elements must clearly make a big contribution. Separate IRD material is being prepared on this and will be issued shortly, and Intel. No 294 has broached the subject already.

(4) Full information on the evidence of this form of Russian imperialism is being currently issued.

Appendix 4
Forced Labour in the Soviet Union

Extracts from C. Mayhew's speech at the Eighth Session of the Economic and Social Council on 15 February 1949

At the last meeting of the General Assembly it was my duty, on behalf of the United Kingdom Delegation, to present a part of the evidence of the existence of mass forced labour in the Soviet Union. Some further evidence has already been given in this debate, and I do not propose now to cover the ground again, nor to quote the fresh evidence which continues to reach the United Kingdom Government on this subject. . . .

On this occasion, I merely wish to draw the attention of the Council to the fact that the inhuman practice of forced labour is now spreading beyond the boundaries of the Soviet Union. We see the evil growing in Czechoslovakia, in Bulgaria and in the Soviet Zone of Germany. We see now that forced labour is not an exclusively Russian phenomenon, it belongs to the practice of communism in several countries. . . .

The anxieties of the free world can be stilled quickly and finally by the Soviet Government. Let them invite representatives of the United Nations, or a group of newspapermen, a representative group, to visit the following areas:-

The great penal area of Karaganda in the Kazakh desert; the concentration of camps at Dalstroi in the Far East, including the coal-mining camp of the Kolyma River; the Pechora group in the north of Europe; the Lake Baikal group in Siberia; the Yagri group in the Arkangel region; and the groups in Lapland, Novaya Zemlya, Sakhalin, Kamchatka and the Novosibirsk, Krasnoyarsk and Arctic regions. Our information shows that these camps include only a fraction of the total forced labour population of the Soviet Union. But visits even to these camps would do much to reassure the outside world.

While, however, access to these camps is refused, while the whole subject of forced labour is kept shrouded in secrecy, the world is bound to continue with its anxieties and suspicions; and the Soviet Government will have only itself to blame for the conclusion which citizens of free countries draw. . . .

Extracts from C. Mayhew's speech to Committee 3 of the UN General Assembly on 4 October 1948

It had been my intention, Mr Chairman, to limit my remarks in this debate to a formal statement of the United Kingdom position, but I feel it would not be appropriate for this debate to end without some reply being made to the highly polemical speech of our Soviet colleague. He struck a discordant note in this debate, which we hoped would be an amicable and cooperative effort to forward the cause of human rights. As in so many other meetings of the United Nations, non-Commmunist countries, among them Britain and the British Commonwealth, found themselves pilloried in the name of democracy by delegates of Communist countries. In our Soviet colleague's speech we were informed that Britain 'holds the branch of domination in her hands'. We were told that we and other members of the Human Rights Commission had been deliberately trying, not to forward, but to obstruct, the case of human rights. Our attitude was described as 'hypocritical'. . . .

Mr Chairman, if we are sincere in our belief in human rights, we cannot remain silent on these issues, and since we are ourselves attacked, we are entitled to speak out about the nature of the political, economic and social freedom of the countries which make the charges against us.

Entirely contrary to the assertions of the Soviet delegation, Communism is one of the most ruthless forms of dictatorship, economic and political, that the world has ever seen. In the democratic countries we are not all ignorant of Marxist-Leninist ideology; we are not just 'dupes of capitalist propaganda'; we are not 'blinded by class

Forced Labour in the Soviet Union

prejudice'. We simply draw plain deductions from observed facts. Let us take first the question of political freedom in these countries. We have heard from more than one delegate from a Communist country of the comprehensive nature of the political rights guaranteed in their Soviet constitutions. Articles of these constitutions have been quoted to us, showing that freedom in all its forms is granted to all in the most specific possible way. Yet even in spite of the secrecy which surrounds these countries, we know beyond doubt that these constitutions are empty shells, that they are not implemented, in fact that they do not confer political rights on the people.

How do we know this, in spite of all the secrecy? Let me quote one fact, which Communist countries have been unable to prevent or conceal – the stream of political refugees to the West. Sometimes it seems to me that the more democratic the form of the constitution of a Communist country, the larger the stream of political refugees. Socialists, democrats, peasant leaders, leaders of anti-Nazi resistance, Trade Unionists, men with fine war records, men who fought with the RAF during the war, men known to us personally, men known to the United Nations – they escape westwards through the bars of the cage. They come in stolen aircraft, in boats, on foot. This is the kind of observed fact which, in the free world, destroys at a blow mountains of Communist propaganda about political freedom.

Let us look at it in the reverse direction. We in the United Kingdom are told that we are the oppressors, the exploiters, and the persecutors. How many British refugees seek asylum in Communist countries? What are the names of those refugees from capitalist-imperialist oppression? In Britain we have no written constitution, none of the fine phrases of the Polish constitution which our Polish delegate quoted to us: but we have more Polish refugees in Britain than there are letters in all the articles of the 'democratic' Polish constitution.

Or, take another aspect of a similar subject – the refusal of the citizens of these countries to return to them. Thousands upon thousands of citizens of Communist countries have refused to return to them since the war. Many are hysterically afraid of returning. In Displaced Persons camps and elsewhere, where citizens of Soviet countries are found, suicide and attempted suicide are preferred to returning to what our Soviet delegate has called the 'fatherland of democracy'.

These are indisputable facts. Were it necessary, and were there time, it would be possible to consider them in greater detail. They are flashes of light which show up the impenetrable darkness behind the Iron Curtain.

Again on the subject of political freedom, we cannot ignore the fact that Communist states, like Hitler's Germany, are one-party states, without legal political opposition. We all know, of course, the Marxist-Leninist explanation of this fact – that political opposition is a reflection of class conflict, and that in Communist countries, since the bourgeoisie has been liquidated and the interests of the workers and peasants coincide, there is no basis for political opposition. This is the thesis presented by M. Pavlov to an early meeting of the Human Rights Committee. What a hopelessly unscientific, even ridiculous explanation for the absence of opposition in Communist states. Even if we make the large assumption that class conflict is the only basis of political opposition, why should we suppose that the interests of workers and peasants coincide? Is collectivisation a non-controversial issue in Communist states? Are the peasants there free to urge their views on collectivisation by democratic methods? Did all the peasants of the Soviet Union agree to collectivisation? Did they all vote unanimously for their own liquidation? How do the formal constitutions we have heard about represent the views of the peasants on this issue?

Are all Communist citizens free to make their views felt on the issues of peace and war? If so, why is there no opposition to Communist foreign policy? Is it because among those missions, not one citizen disagrees? Do all those millions agree together on Monday that a certain country is a 'People's Democracy', and then all agree together on Tuesday that it is governed by a group of political adventurers? It is plainly contrary to common-sense. The truth is, of course, that on the vital issues of peace and war, citizens of a Communist country are prevented, despite their fine-sounding constitutions, from making their views felt.

Or let us take the case of individual rights. It happens that we know of the case of certain Soviet wives of British nationals, who, at least before pressure was put on them, stated that they wished to join their husbands in Britain. How did the Soviet constitution operate in this case? Which delegates at which District Soviet took the part of these women? How were their views heard? In which free Soviet newspaper was their point-of-view published? Or can it be that the Soviet constitution in fact gave these women no rights whatsoever, any more than it gives rights to any Soviet citizens who suffer oppression and injustice? It happens by unusual circumstances that we know of these particular cases. Throughout the length and breadth of Communist countries there must be millions of individuals, voiceless, without rights, without means of redress, to whom these high-sounding Soviet constitutions are a mockery of freedom.

In Communist states, there are no opposition deputies, no opposition newspapers, no opposition votes, no opposition speeches, no opposition broadcasts, no opposition scientists, no opposition writers, no opposition biologists, no opposition musicians – just a uniform desert of Communist dictatorship. And the reason is not, as the Marxist-Leninists allege, because there is no basis for opposition, but because, for reasons of power, opposition is suppressed by the Communist parties and their secret police. . . .

Extracts from C. Mayhew's Speech to Committee 3 of the UN General Assembly on 15 October 1948

Mr Chairman, the Committee will recall that in yesterday's proceedings the Soviet Delegate, in moving his amendment made an unprovoked and very outspoken attack on the subject of lynching in [the] United States of America and alleged colonial exploitation by [the] United Kingdom. He received, what was, if I may say so, a brief, temperate and courteous reply from Mrs Roosevelt; and from myself, in the interest of the work of the Committee, no direct reply at all.

Both of us hoped, I think, that our restraint would be rewarded. But our reward was a still lengthier, more savage act of verbal aggression from our Soviet Colleague. My own failure to reply was ascribed as not to patience or restraint, or respect for the Committee, but to a total

Appendix 4

incapacity to produce facts to refute the allegations made.

The Soviet Delegate argued that his amendment made it the duty of a State 'to ensure conditions that obviated the danger of death by hunger and exhaustion'; and that this amendment was necessary in order to prevent alleged conditions of colonial oppression existing in the British Commonwealth, which, he alleged caused the death, by starvation or malnutrition of millions of British subjects. In support of his thesis he quoted a number of mortality rates. . . .

Mr Chairman, since we in the United Kingdom have been twice attacked on this amendment in this Committee by the Soviet Delegate and have not replied, we are surely entitled to enquire what moral right our critics have to make these allegations against us. I repeat what I have said before in this Committee, that I believe our work would be done better harmoniously. But there are times when in reply to provocation, it is moral cowardice to remain silent. The subject of forced labour in the Soviet Union is not a new one. . . .

Since 1930 when these things were being considered, and particularly since 1939, we have learnt some terrible lessons. The suspicions which the opponents of Nazism held about German concentration camps were more than confirmed by the revelations which followed the defeat of Hitler. With that confirmation, came a better realisation of how a totalitarian or one-party state can conceal facts inconvenient to itself not only from the outside world, but from its own people, and even from members of its own administration up to a very high level. We have learnt too that when a system of depriving large numbers of people of their liberty by police methods is instituted, it runs away with itself. When one concentration camp is established, another follows, and we have found that the staffs and administrations of these camps, unchecked by the continual searchlight of publicity, indulge in increasing brutality, while the impetus of the police force which collects the unfortunate inhabitants of these camps is for the same reason unrestrained. It can no longer be denied that the Soviet Union is making use of large numbers of prisoners as forced labour in conditions denying to them the basic human rights; that these human beings, once deprived of their liberty, are maintained in conditions of wretchedness and undernourishment; that under the cloak of arrest for crimes and other offences against the regime, the Soviet Government has acquired for itself a vast body of cheap labour utterly without rights. That, in short, the Soviet Union has instituted a slave system recruited from among its own citizens which in scope has no parallel in history. . . .

In 1931 a leading Soviet authority spoke of mass projects employing those deprived of liberty. This authority was none other than Mr Molotov. Mr Molotov, who was then Chairman of the USSR Council of People's Commissars, was addressing the Sixth Congress of Soviets. He said, I quote: 'These mass projects employing those deprived of liberty are organised for a variety of different objectives; for highway construction, in particular on railways, in the building industry, in peat exploitation, in charcoal burning for metallurgical plants, in timber works, in phosphorite mining, stone quarries, gravel and stone crushing, on transportation projects, etc.' . . .

In 1934 Mr Vyshinsky compiled a book called *From Prisons to Educational Institutions*. Mr Stelmalch, one of the writers in the book, said that in 1931 294,015 copies of Soviet newspapers were sent to, I quote: 'All places of detention' in the RSFSR, some 60,000 to the Ukraine and 11,713 to Byelorussia. That makes a total of 365,000. In the same book Mr Shestakova says that an average five inmates received one newspaper. A simple enough act of multiplication has suggested to students of the subject a total in the areas I have mentioned of 1,830,000 prisoners in 1931. This is, of course, a tentative figure. It is, however, one quoted. It is several millions less than any estimate made by non-Soviet sources. . . .

Red Forced Labour by Mr Kikonov Smorodin was published in Sofia in 1938. The author, who escaped from the camp, estimates the total to be between five and six millions for the period 1935 to 1937. *La Justice Sovietique* compiled by Mr Moore and Mr Svernik is a collective work based on a multitude of reports from former Polish prisoners. It was published in Rome in 1945. It lists 31 names of labour camps and gives an estimate of 15,000,000 inmates for the years 1940 to 1942. The estimate of a Soviet Army colonel, Lieutenant Colonel G. A. Tokaev who recently arrived in Britain after a life-time service in the Soviet regime, sometimes in positions of considerable authority, is that

Appendix 4

there are 13 million slave labourers in the USSR. ...

Mr Chairman, if the great body of evidence on Soviet Forced Labour, that is now available to us has any meaning at all, it means that there exists in Soviet Russia a monstrous system of oppression, which makes a mockery of the claim that that country is a democratic or a socialist state. It bears out the truth – that for democrats, socialists and working men and women the world over Soviet Russia provides not an example, but a deadly warning.

Mr Chairman, a great deal more could be said about this question, and a great deal more evidence produced. The free world is asking questions about the Soviet Forced Labour camps. We ask – are all these reports, from so many different sources, wholly false? Above all, we ask – if there is nothing to hide, why the silence and secrecy? If we are wrong, let the truth be known. Until then, we deny the moral right of Soviet propagandists to attack our freedom and deride our democratic ways. If the Soviet spokesmen wish to persist in their attacks on human rights, the British Commonwealth and the countries of the West, let them grant us the same right of access to their country as we grant them to ours. Let them publish, as we do, all the facts and figures of success and failure in the field of social advancement. Until then, Mr Chairman, we deny that they have the moral right to make their repeated, unprovoked, unsubstantiated allegations against us.

Appendix 5
Letter Christopher Mayhew to Mr A. A. Arutiunian, 31 October 1947

I was sorry to have to come home so soon from [the] UN, leaving our various arguments in the air. It was most refreshing to discuss familiar controversies with someone experienced in the practice as well as the theory of communism. So many of our 'Western' communists know only the theory of the thing – and most of our British communists are so brainless as not to know even that!

I doubt if either of us will ever persuade the other of anything! But I propose to write to you a long and persuasive letter in the hope – a very faint hope – that I may possibly contrive to sow some seeds of doubt in your mind.

As I tried to explain during our talks, I think that the basic fallacy of most Soviet thinking comes from the application of Marxist-Leninist hypotheses in too rigid and uncritical a form. Your famous self-criticism is always applied within the bounds of your Marxist-Leninist dogmas. You allow yourselves too seldom to turn your sharp intelligences upon the dogmas themselves, and their relevance to the objective facts which you are studying. For example, the broad Marxist thesis that the state machine is the instrument of the ruling class is well understood in the West. I was taught about it at my university – it is part of the normal curriculum. Every sociologist in Britain is familiar with Marx's and Lenin's writings. Marxism is not new or challenging to us – it is old and familiar. Like Darwinism, it has left its mark on our intellectual climate, and has helped to form our ways of thought. But it is of course years and years since Darwin and Marx did their pioneering work, and I think that no one would be

Appendix 5

more horrified than they at the kind of application sometimes made of their hypotheses today.

For example – it is now 100 years since the publication of the *Communist Manifesto*. The writings of Freud, Planck and Einstein have intervened – to name only a few revolutions in modern thought. Now in 1848 Marx's interpretation of the British democracy as a sham, a concealed dictatorship of the bourgeoisie, was pretty shrewd and accurate. At any rate it was a fairer interpretation than that of contemporary bourgeois political science. In those days the Government was, more or less, the instrument of our all-powerful industrialists and landed interests. The proletariat, oppressed and badly paid, showed in the 'hungry 40s' (1844–8 particularly) the corresponding degree of revolutionary spirit, such as any good sociologist would expect. On one occasion, the workers formed a mass demonstration nearly 2 million strong, and there were a number of broken heads, and even a small and unsuccessful insurrection. That was the British bourgeois democracy 100 years ago – shrewdly described and exposed by Marx in his early days. And if the same or similar conditions existed in Britain today, or were ever likely to exist, I assure you that I should be the first to join the British Communist Party. But few of us would be so naive as to expect at any time in the future the same social conditions, or class relations, as in the dark days of Britain's industrial predominance *100 years ago*. There could be no greater error of political analysis than to apply to British social-democracy today, the same interpretation and predictions as Marx and Lenin made about our bourgeois democracy many years ago. British and foreign communists make this mistake. For example, when they look on the British Labour Party as 'Mensheviks' – due to give way to a 'genuine revolutionary' workers' movement at some future date. I assure you that these people will have a long time to wait! The economic relations do not exist for such a revolution, and there is no reason whatever why they ever should exist in the future. Every trend is in the reverse direction – not towards the sharpening of class conflict but towards the disappearance of such remnants of class friction as still remain in this country after 100 years of democratisation. We have already nationalised the following industries – the Bank of England, Coal, Electricity, Road Transport,

Letter Christopher Mayhew to Mr A. A. Arutiunian

Civil Aviation, International Tele-communications and the Railways. This coming Session we shall nationalise the gas industry and, after that, iron and steel. We are drastically redistributing wealth, and shall continue to do so. We have already democratised education to a great extent, and have further plans for it. Economic and social distinction between the proletariat and bourgeoisie are rapidly being levelled out. Wages have risen. There is no destitution in Britain. The workers are not oppressed and do not feel oppressed. Their own chosen representatives are in key positions in the Government.

And yet – and yet – we still have the same old story from you and your fellow communists about the 'power of British monopoly capitalism' and 'the betrayal of the workers by the servile Labour Government'. We are described as 'lackeys' and 'social Fascists' in the new Cominform declaration. Of course I do not mind a bit myself being insulted in this way – I have been attacked by communists for 10 years and more now, and am growing 'thick skinned'! What *does* distress and alarm me is the faulty political analysis which lies behind these attacks, since it is this faulty analysis which is, in my view, at the root of the disastrous errors of Soviet foreign policy. It is this faulty analysis which leads you to jump to conclusions about the inevitable hostility of the West towards Russia. But the truth is that the hostility which exists is due not to 'the sinister power of the monopoly capitalists' so much as to the very natural resentment and suspicion which wild and ill-informed Soviet attacks make on ordinary citizens – myself included – belonging to all social and economic classes in the Western democracies. Any nation and any person who expects to be hated in the world, and therefore acts suspiciously and sometimes aggressively – is bound to end up by being hated and feared. If it was not for this faulty Marxist analysis, communists would know that the overwhelming majority of people in the Western countries of all economic classes want peace and friendship with Soviet Russia. What restrains the masses in Europe and America from trusting and respecting Soviet Russia, is not so much their economic interests (very few of them are 'monopoly capitalists!'), nor the 'lying propaganda of the capitalist press', but the behaviour and policy of Soviet Russia herself.

Why do you not make a real effort to re-examine the fundamentals

Appendix 5

of your thought? Why do you not allow in Soviet Russia writers and thinkers to criticise your Marxist ideology, as well allow Marxists to criticise our ways of thought? In that way truth is born, and the way towards agreement becomes clearer.

As it is, you cling to your old hypotheses as though your lives depended on them! You have come to the position familiar to all scientists – either you must modify your hypotheses, or else you must cling to them and select your verifying facts. Soviet Russia appears to be choosing the second course. Selection of facts to support preconceived hypotheses is the feature of all communist propaganda throughout the world. Ask any scientist where that path leads to!

I could go on dictating this letter for an indefinite period of time. It is only the beginning of the case. I feel sure that you will not mind my frank speaking. I only hope that you will manage to find time to reply some day in the same spirit.

With my best wishes.

Yours sincerely

C. P. Mayhew

P.S. I need hardly add that in all this letter I am speaking confidentially, for myself, and not in an official way.

Bibliography

Benn, Tony, *Against The Tide: Diaries 1973–76* (Century Hutchinson, London, 1989)

Bower, Tom, *Robert Maxwell: The Final Verdict* (Harper Collins, New York, 1996)

Gaddis, J. L., *We Now Know: Rethinking Cold War History* (Clarendon Press, Oxford, 1997)

Halliday, Fred, *The Making of the Second Cold War* (Verso, London, 1983)

Hobsbawm, Eric, *Age of Extremes: The Short Twentieth Century 1914-1991* (Michael Joseph Ltd, London, 1994)

Hollander, P., *Political Pilgrims: Travels of Western Intellectuals to the Soviet Union, China and Cuba 1928–78* (Oxford University Press, Oxford, 1981)

Howard, A., *Crossman: The Pursuit of Power* (Jonathan Cape, London, 1990)

Jones, M., *Michael Foot* (Victor Gollancz, London, 1994)

Mayhew, Christopher, *Time to Explain: An Autobiography* (Century Hutchinson, London, 1987)

Lebow, N. and Stein, J., *We All Lost the Cold War* (Princeton University Press, New Jersey, 1994)

Morgan, Kevin, *Harry Pollitt* (Manchester University Press, Manchester, 1993)

Orwell, George, *The Road to Wigan Pier* (Victor Gollancz, London, 1937)

Reynolds, D., *The Origins of the Cold War in Europe: International Perspectives* (Yale University Press, Boston, 1994)

Smith, Lyn, 'Covert British Propaganda: The Information Research Department 1947–1977', *Millennium: Journal of International Studies*, vol. 9, no. 1, 1980

Volkogonov, Dimitri, *Lenin: Life and Legacy* (Harper Collins, New York, 1994)

Bibliography

Volkov, Solomon, *Testimony: The Memoirs of Shostakovich* (Hamish Hamilton, London, 1979)

Cabinet Paper CAB (48) 8, 4 January 1948

Foreign Office documents referred to in the text were taken from the author's personal archive. This is now being catalogued and is housed in the Liddell Hart Foundation, King's College, London. These papers should also be available from the Public Records Office, Kew under the class number FO371.

In 1995, the first batch of IRD papers was released, with further releases following at regular intervals. Those pertaining to the year 1948 are in class FO1110, piece numbers 1–165.

Index

Adams, Mr Grantley, 35, 117n8
Adenauer, Konrad, 116
Afghanistan, 45
Aitken, Dr R. S., 73
Ampersand Ltd, 29
Andropov, Yuri, 111–13
Anglo-Soviet Trade Treaty, 38
Armenia, 17, 37
Arutiunian, Amazap, 17, 36–7, 39, 137
Ashdown, Paddy, 95
Asia, 31, 34, 36, 104, 124, 128
Athens, 104
Atlantic Pact, 33, 80
Attlee, Clement, 8, 13, 19, 21, 25, 39–40, 58, 67, 74, 83, 103–4, 115
Austria, 21
Ayer, Professor A. J., 7, 56

Barbados, 35, 117n8
Bavaria, 13
BBC, 21, 28–31, 37, 41, 44, 49, 57, 59, 61, 78, 90, 92, 105, 124
Beaverbrook, Lord, 16, 71
Belgrade, 29
Belorussia, 35
Benn, Tony, 90, 108–10
Beria, Lavrenti, 49, 67
Berkeley, George, 7
Berlin, 26, 39, 83, 107
Bevan, Aneurin, 22–3, 39
Bevin, Ernest, 13–15, 18–19, 21–6, 28–9, 32–3, 38–42, 64, 83, 115, 120
Birmingham, 90
Bliss, Sir Arthur, 68
Blunt, Anthony, 3, 5–6, 100
Blunt, Wilfrid, 5–6
Bogatyrev, Mr, 68
Bolshoi, 69
Bolshoi Ballet, 75–6
Bosphorus, 100
Bournemouth, 95, 114
British Communist Party, 52, 101, 114, 138

British Council, 57–8, 60, 68, 71, 73–5, 78
British Youth Festival Committee, 52, 70
British–East/West Centre, 74
British–Russian Centre, 74
British–Soviet Friendship Society (BSFS), 51–2, 60, 63, 68, 72
Britten, Benjamin, 58, 79
Brook, Norman, 46
Brown, George, 82, 88
Brussels, 9, 33, 81
Bulganin, Marshal Nikolay, 59, 60–3, 113
Burgess, Guy, 5–6, 24, 67, 98, 100
Burns, Robert, 58

Cairncross, John, 100
Callaghan, James, 38, 82, 88
Cambridge, 3
Campaign for Democratic Socialism (CDS), 82
Campaign for Multilateral Disarmament (CMD), 82, 83, 85
Campaign for Nuclear Disarmament (CND), 82, 84–7, 96–7
CBS, 37, 49
Ceylon, 34, 123
Chambers, Revd George, 104
Charles, Sir Noel, 100
Chequers, 21
Chiang Kai-shek, 83
China, 105–6; Indo-China, 123
Chipp, David, 106
Christ Church, 7–8
Christ Church Socialist Study Group, 8
Churchill, Winston, 39, 112
cold war, 14, 40, 43–4, 50–9, 63, 66, 71, 78, 99, 104, 111–12, 115–16
Collins, Canon John, 86, 88
Colonial Information Policy Committee, 42
Colonial Office, 31–2
Cominform, 18, 53–6, 81, 116, 121, 125, 139
Comintern, 10, 55, 101, 116
Common Market referendum, 46
Commons, House of, 25–6, 100, 104

Index

Commonwealth, 31, 33, 122, 124–5, 127, 130, 134, 136
Commonwealth Relations Office, 31
Communist International, 9, 70
Communist Party, 5, 9, 44, 54, 60, 64, 88, 92, 99–104, 108; *see also* British Communist Party
Compton, 6
Conquest, Robert, 29
Council of Europe, 78, 92
Council of Foreign Ministers (CFM), 19–21, 121
Cousins, Frank, 82
Covent Garden, 62, 66
Cox, Dr John, 96–7
Crawley, Aidan, 106
Cripps, Sir Stafford, 38
Crosland, Tony, 12
Crossman, Dick, 19–20, 25, 39, 85–6
Crowther, Mr J. G., 80–1
Crozier, Brian, 29
Cruickshank, Andrew, 48–9
Cuban missile crisis, 40, 92
Czechoslovakia, 25, 112, 116, 129

Daily Express, 71
Daily Mail, 27
Daily Telegraph, 27
Daily Worker, 44, 49, 52
Deakin, Arthur, 41
Dean, Pat, 46
Descartes, René, 7
Dicks, Dr H. V., 42
Doctors for Peace, 81
Dorril, Mr Stephen, 43, 44
Douglas-Home, Sir Alec, 78, 90
Dowlais, 10
Driberg, Tom, 66–7, 100
Dundee, Earl of, 89

East Europe Committee, 78
Eastbourne, 97
Economic and Social Council, 16, 36, 48, 129
Economist, 27, 73
Eden, Anthony, 62–3, 67
Egypt, 57
Encounter, 84
Etheridge, Dick, 108

Far East Department, 24

Feather, Vic, 29, 75
Financial Times, 27
Finsbury, 103
First World War, 56, 116
Foot, Michael, 19, 25, 85, 88, 94
Foreign Office, 13, 14, 17, 23–4, 27, 29–31, 38, 42–3, 46, 48, 57–9, 67–8, 70, 73–5, 89, 99, 104, 124, 127, 128, 142
Forrest, William, 28
Foster, Michael, 6–7
Foulkes, Mr, 46
Franco, General Francisco, 83
Fraser, Sir Robert, 106
Freedom First, 41
Furtseva, Madame, 76, 86

Gaitskell, Hugh, 77, 82, 85–6, 88, 90, 93–4
Geneva Gazette, 36
German Social Democratic Party, 13, 101, 107
Germany, 20, 102, 107, 113–14, 115–16, 121, 129, 132
Gibraltar, 83
Gladwyn Jebb (later Lord Gladwyn), 33
Goldberg, Anatole, 30
Gorbachev, Mikhail, 93, 97
Gordievsky, Oleg, 104, 112
Gordon Walker, Patrick, 31–2, 42
Gorki market, 51
Gott, Mr Richard, 43–4, 96, 104
Great Britain–USSR Association, 74
Greece, 14–15, 22, 36, 107, 116, 121
Greene, Felix, 105–6
Greene, Sir Hugh, 30, 46
Greenwood, Tony, 85
Gromeka, Mr, 72
Gromyko, Andrei Andreevich, 40, 53–5
Guardian, 27, 43–4, 89–90, 95–7, 104, 114
Gulag, 35

Haileybury, 1, 5
Harrison, Tony, 45
Harrod, Roy, 6
Haxell, Mr, 46
Healey, Denis, 40, 82
Heathrow, 59, 75
Helsinki, 81, 112
Henderson, Arthur, 83
Hendy, Sir Philip, 68
Hill, Charles, 69, 71, 106
Hiss, Alger, 107

Index

Hitler, Adolf, 12–13, 21, 44, 100–1, 126, 132, 134
Hohler, Harry, 58
Hollis, Mr (later Sir) Roger, 46, 98
Home Counties, 10
Hong Kong, 31
Howard, Sir Michael, 113
Hughes, Emrys, 25
Human Rights Commission, 16, 130
Hume, David, 7
Hungary, 45, 65–9, 116
Hurd, Douglas, 23, 77

Imperial Defence College, 99
Independent, 114
India, 33–4, 59, 123
Indonesia, 46, 123
Information Research Department (IRD), 23–4, 25–35, 40–1, 43–7, 81, 89–90, 92, 100, 104, 120, 128, 141–2
International Union of Students (IUS), 70
Intourist, 1–2, 100
Iron Curtain, 24, 30, 72, 128, 132
Iskra, 114
Isle of Wight, 25
Israel, 41, 83
ITV, 105–6

Jacob, Sir Ian, 30, 57–8
Jacobs, Sir Anthony, 111
Janner, Barnett, 77
Jay, Douglas, 82
Jenkins, Roy, 12, 93
Johnson, Dr Hewlett, 51
Johnson, Sir Russell, 111

Kant, Immanuel, 7
Karachi, 34, 45
Kautsky, Karl, 115
Kennedy, President John, 115
Kent, Bruce, 96–7
Keynes, John Maynard, 6
KGB, 24, 37, 44, 48, 67, 77, 96, 99–101, 104–5, 111–12
Khrushchev, Nikita, 59–64, 88–9, 92
Kirkpatrick, Mr Ivone, 19, 23, 26
Kommunist, 92
Komsomolskaya Pravda, 71
Königswinter, 113
Korea, North, 55, 80; South, 55, 80–1

Korionov, Vitaly, 92
Kremlin, 3, 49, 50, 114–15
Kryuchkov, Vladimir, 77

Labour Club, 8–10, 12
Labour Party, 6, 11–13, 28, 31, 40, 42, 45, 66–7, 72–3, 76, 82–3, 84–5, 87–8, 93–4, 103, 107–10, 125, 138; *see also* Parliamentary Labour Party
Lancaster House, 20
Laski, Harold, 8
Latin America, 104
Law, Dick, 53, 54–5
League of Nations, 107
Lebow, Ned, 115–16
Lenin, Vladimir Ilyich, 7–8, 40, 50–1, 54, 56, 93, 99, 101, 106, 110, 112, 114–16, 130, 132–3, 137–8
Leningrad, 1–2, 6
Liaquat, Ali Khan, 34
Liberal Party, 10, 93–7, 111, 113–14
Literary Gazette, 64–5
Llandudno, 95
Locke, John, 7
London Bridge, 1
Longden, Gilbert, 74, 78
Lords, House of, 89
Ludlam, Cicely, 36

McDonald, Malcolm, 34
Mackenzie, Archie, 38
Maclean, Donald, 100
Maclean, Sir Fitzroy, 73–4
Macmillan, Harold, 116
McNeil, Hector, 16, 24, 38, 67, 103
Malay Mail, 46
Malaya, 31, 46, 80–1, 123
Malenkov, Georgiy, 49–50
Malik, Jacob, 60, 72–3, 75
Manchester, 11
Manchester Guardian, 107
Marcuse, Jacques, 105
Marshall Plan, 38–9, 42, 46, 122
Martin, Kingsley, 85
Marx, Karl, 8, 101, 137–9
Marxism, 4, 6–8, 17, 37, 40, 51–3, 55–7, 65, 75, 79, 80, 88–93, 99, 104, 108–10, 112, 115–16, 121, 130, 132–3, 137–40
Maxwell, Robert, 76–7
Mayevsky, Victor, 90–2

145

Index

Metropole Hotel, 2
MI5, 5, 24, 46, 98–100, 103
Michawowski, 14
Middle East, 92, 121, 123–5
Mikardo, Ian, 107
Mikhailov, Mr, 58–61, 76
Mitty, Walter, 62
Moiseyev ensemble, 59–61
Molotov, Vyacheslav, 15–16, 20–1, 26, 39, 50, 53, 55, 135
Montagu, Mr Ivor, 52
Morrison, Herbert, 13, 39
Moscow, 1–3, 6, 18, 52, 57, 63–70, 73–7, 81, 88, 90, 92, 100, 111, 113–14
Moscow Circus, 63
Moscow State Theatre, 79
Moscow Youth Festival, 52, 70
Mosley, Gordon, 49
Mott-Radclyffe, C. E., 58, 74
Munich, 13
Murray, Mr (later Sir) Ralph, 24, 32
Mussolini, Benito, 100

Napoleon I, 56–7
Nation, 85
National Union of Teachers, 72
NATO, 26, 33, 39, 83, 94–6, 113
Nazism, 10–11, 100–2, 131, 134
Nehru, Jawaharlal, 33–4
Nenk, David, 1–4, 117n1
New Delhi, 33
New Statesman, 85
New York, 16–17
New York Times, 36
News, 60
News Chronicle, 28
News of the World, 27
Nicosia, 104
Noel-Baker, Mrs, 15
Noel-Baker, Philip, 15, 82
Norfolk, 12–13, 103
North Africa, 24
North Atlantic Assembly, 114
Nye, Sir Archibald, 33

Observer, 27–8, 102
October Club, 8
October Revolution, 70, 105
Oistrakh, David, 58
Ormsby Gore, David, 73

Orwell, George, 106
Owen, Dr David, 46, 94–5
Oxford, 3–4, 8–10, 12, 31, 102, 115
Oxford and Cambridge Club, 5
Oxford Union, 3, 10, 102
Oxford University Democratic Socialist Group, 8–9

Pakistan, 33–4, 45
Paris, 46, 108
Parliamentary Labour Party, 12, 14, 24–5, 90, 98–9
Peking, 31, 83, 106
Pergamon, 77
Persia, 14–15
Peru, 16
Peshawar, 45
Philby, Kim, 24, 100
Phillips, Morgan, 13
Pilcher, John, 31
Platts-Mills, Mr John, 61, 103
Points at Issue, 28, 42
Poland, 28
Politburo, 49, 93
Pollitt, Harry, 5, 101–2
Pravda, 90
Preston, Peter, 96
Pritt, D. N., 51, 103

Queen Elizabeth, 16, 18
Queen Mary, 39

Radio Moscow, 92
Reagan, Ronald, 111, 113, 116
Reddaway, Mr Norman, 24, 46
Rees-Mogg, William, 110
Rees-Williams, David, 31
Reuters, 106
Reynolds News, 66–7
Rogers, Bill, 82, 88
Rome, 46, 135
Roosevelt, Eleanor, 34, 133
Roschin, Mr, 77
Russell, Bertrand, 29, 56, 84, 94
Russia, 1–3, 6, 14, 16–17, 19–22, 24, 28, 31, 33, 36, 38–9, 50–6, 58, 60–2, 65, 67–71, 73–4, 79, 86, 102–4, 114, 122–4, 126–9, 136, 139–40; *see also* Soviet Union; USSR
Russia Committee, 30, 42

Index

Ryan, 111–13, 116

Sadler's Wells Ballet, 65–7
St Petersburg, 56
Sapper, Alan, 110
Sargent, Sir Orme, 19, 23
Scarborough, 82
Scientists for Peace, 81
Scofield, Paul, 76
Selwyn Lloyd, John, 61–3
Seton Watson, Hugh, 29
Shaw, George Bernard, 101
Sheffield, 80–1
Sheffield Telegraph, 80
Shepherd, Mr George, 12
Shevardnadze, Eduard, 93
Shostakovich, Dmitri, 75, 79
Singapore, 34
Sinker, Sir Paul, 58, 68, 73–4
Slessor, Air Marshal, 99
Sloan, Pat, 51
Social Democratic Party (Bavaria), 13
Social Democratic Party (SDP), 94–5
Socialist Unity Party, 13
Society for Cultural Relations (SCR), 52, 61, 68–9, 72
Sokolovsky, Marshall, 20
Solzhenitsyn, Alexander, 35
South Norfolk, 12–13, 103
Soviet Analyst, 27
Soviet Relations Committee (SRC), 59–62, 65, 67–78
Soviet Union, 1–6, 12, 15–19, 21–2, 24, 26–8, 31–2, 33–40, 42, 44–5, 47–78, 80–1, 83, 86, 90–3, 95, 98–106, 111–16, 121, 124–6, 128, 129–37, 139–40; *see also* Russia; USSR
Soviet Writers' Union, 58
Spaak, Monsieur, 33
Spain, 102, 116
Stacey, Nicholas, 88
Stalin, Joseph, 2–5, 12, 14–18, 26, 29, 42, 47, 49–50, 52, 64, 67, 80, 88, 98–100, 102–3, 107, 114–15
Stalinism/Stalinist, 2–5, 9–10, 17, 25, 27, 33, 40–1, 43, 47, 64, 67–8, 104–5
Stanley, Sydney, 41
Stanstead, 75–6
Star, 78
State Committee for Cultural Relations with Foreign Countries, 58

Steel, David, 94–5, 111–12
Stein, Janice, 115–16
Strachey, John, 8, 85
Stratford-on-Avon, 76
Sukarno, Achmed, 46
Sunday Mirror, 27
Sunday Telegraph, 27
Sunday Times, 27–8
Surkov, Mr, 58
Surrey, 6
Sutherland, Sir Iain, 113

Tass, 3
Territorial Army, 12
Tewson, Vincent, 41, 58, 75
Third World, 18, 20, 35, 47, 89, 92
Times, The, 27–8, 45, 65, 68, 71, 94, 114
Tito, Marshal, 29, 55
Tolstoy, Count Leo Nikolayevich, 58
Toynbee, Philip, 102
Tracey, Herbert, 41
Transport and General Workers' Union, 82
Trevor-Roper, Hugh (later Lord Dacre), 29
Tripp, Miss Brenda, 75
Truman, President Harry, 15
TUC, 41
Turkey, 15
Turton, Robin, 57

Ukraine, 35, 135
Ulanova, Galina, 76
United Nations (UN), 15–19, 34–7, 40–2, 47, 48, 70, 120–2, 129–31, 133, 137
United States of America, 14–15, 17–18, 21–3, 31–2, 34–5, 37–8, 42, 49, 55, 80–2, 92, 111, 113–16, 121–3, 125, 127, 133, 139
University Labour Federation (ULF), 11–12
Urban, Dr George, 30
US Congress, 14
USSR, 30, 36, 65, 74, 104, 135–6; *see also* Russia; Soviet Union

Vassall, Mr, 100
Vienna, 71, 104
Vietnam, 81
Vilensky, M., 65
Vyshinsky, Andrey, 15–17, 20, 135

Wales, 10
War Office, 42

Index

Warner, Mr C. F. A., 19, 32–3
Warsaw, 24
Warsaw Pact, 113
Washington, 24, 32, 38, 100
Waterloo, battle of, 57
Watson, Jock, 103
Watts, Stephen, 29
Watts' Gallery, 6
Webb, Sidney and Beatrice, 4, 101
Wehrmacht, 42
Wellesley, Gerald, 56
Western European Union, 26, 39
Westminster, 43, 45, 83
Williamson, Tom, 41

Wilson, Harold, 31, 86, 88, 93, 95
World Assembly of Youth, 70
World Federation of Democratic Youth (WFDY), 70, 81
World Federation of Trade Unions (WFTU), 41, 81
World Peace Council, 80–1
Wright, Mr Peter, 5, 98

Yakovlev, Mr V., 65
Young Pioneers, 4

Zhukov, Mr, 58
Zilliacus, Konni, 51, 107–8

www.ingramcontent.com/pod-product-compliance
Lightning Source LLC
Chambersburg PA
CBHW071152020526
44117CB00043B/2044